Publishing Details

This first edition published November 2001 by
The Tipbook Company bv, The Netherlands.

Distributed exclusively by the Hal Leonard Corporation,
7777 West Bluemound Road, P.O. Box 13819
Milwaukee, Wisconsin 53213.

Typeset in Glasgow and Minion.

Printed in The Netherlands by Hentenaar Boek bv, Nieuwegein.

144pp

ISBN 90-76192-46-4

Hugo Pinksterboer

Tipbook
Clarinet

Handy, clearly written, and up-to-date.
The reference manual for both beginning and advanced
clarinet players, including a clarinetist's glossary.

THE **TIPBOOK** COMPANY

THE BEST GUIDE TO YOUR INSTRUMENT!

Thanks

For their information, their expertise, their time, and their help we'd like to thank the following musicians, teachers, technicians and other clarinet experts: Rose Sperrazza (International Clarinet Association), Terry Landry (Rico International), François Kloc (Buffet Crampon, USA), James Grondin (Woodwind & Brasswind), Linda and Bill Brannen (Brannen Woodwinds), Mrs. Wurlitzer (Herbert Wurlitzer, Germany), Aaron McEvers, Jerry Hall (Leblanc, USA), Mr. Hammerschmidt (Hammerschmidt, Germany), Herman Braune (Conservatory of Amsterdam), Lute Hoekstra, Walter Boeykens (Conservatories of London, Antwerp, and Rotterdam), Eddy Vanoosthuyse, Gaby Kerrmann and Rupert Naumann (Schreiber woodwind instruments, Germany), John de Beer and Coen Wolfgram (NERV: Dutch Single Reed Association), Wouter Bierenbroodspot, Henri Bok (Conservatory of Rotterdam), Rijmert Goppel, Dr. Harm van der Geest, Maarten Jense, Bas de Jong (Residentie Orkest, Conservatory of Utrecht), Koos van Nieuwkasteele, Marianne Poelhekken, Hein Pijnenburg, Henk Rensink, Jos Ruiters, Bert Steinmann, Karin Vrieling (*De Klarinet*), René Wiggers, Pieter Bukkems and Ton Minnen (JIC/Leblanc), Richard Boerstra, Aad Contze (BIN/Selmer), Piet Jeegers (Piet Jeegers mouthpieces), Frits de Jong (Boosey & Hawkes/Buffet Crampon), Gerard Koning (Yamaha), Ton Kooiman, Leo van Oostrom, Martin Schaap, Han van Schaik, and Casper van der Spek.

We also wish to thank everyone at JIC (Leblanc), Muller, and Yamaha for supplying instruments and further assistance, and Maartje Peek for her musical help in making the cover and the Tipcode-movies.

Anything missing?

Any omissions? Any areas that could be improved? Please go to www.tipbook.com to contact us; thanks!

Acknowledgements

Concept, design, and illustrations: Gijs Bierenbroodspot

Cover photo: René Vervloet

Translation: MdJ Copy & Translation

Editor: Robert L. Doerschuk

Proofreaders: Nancy Bishop and René de Graaff

IN BRIEF

Have you just started to play the clarinet? Are you thinking about buying a clarinet, or do you just want to find out more about the one you already have? If so, this book will tell you all you need to know. About buying or renting clarinets, about wooden and plastic instruments, about bores and barrels, reeds, and mouthpieces, about tuning and maintenance, about the clarinet's history and the members of the clarinet family, and much more besides.

The best you can

Having read this Tipbook, you'll be able to get the most out of your clarinet, to buy the best instrument you can, and to easily grasp any other literature on the subject, from magazines to books and Internet publications.

Begin at the beginning

If you have just started playing, or haven't yet begun, pay particular attention to the first four chapters. Have you been playing longer? Then skip ahead to Chapter 5. Please note that all prices mentioned in this book are mere indications of street prices in US dollars.

Glossary

The glossary at the end of the book briefly explains most of the terms you'll come across as a clarinet player. To make life even easier, it doubles as an index.

Hugo Pinksterboer

CONTENTS

SEE WHAT YOU READ WITH TIPCODE

www.tipbook.com

In addition to the many illustrations on the following pages, Tipbooks offer you an additional way to see – and even hear – what you are reading about. The *Tipcodes* that you will come across regularly in this book give you access to extra pictures, short movies, soundtracks, and other additional information at www.tipbook.com.

How it works is very simple. One example: On page 80 of this book you can read about the best way to adjust the underside of a reed. Right above that paragraph it says **Tipcode CLR-010**. Type in that code on the Tipcode page at www.tipbook.com and you will see a short movie that shows you this technique.

Enter code, watch movie
You enter the Tipcode beneath the movie window on the Tipcode page. In most cases, you will then see the relevant images within five to ten seconds. Tipcodes activate a short movie, sound, or both, or a series of photos.

Tipcodes listed
To make it easy, you can find all the Tipcodes used in this book in a single list on page 128.

Quick start
The movies, photo series, and sound tracks are designed so that they start quickly. If you miss something the first time, you can of course repeat them. And if it all happens too fast, use the pause button beneath the movie window.

First, make your selection: Tipcode, chords and fingering charts, or the glossary.

The Tipcode window displays movies, photo series, fingering charts, chords, and explanations of the words used in this book.

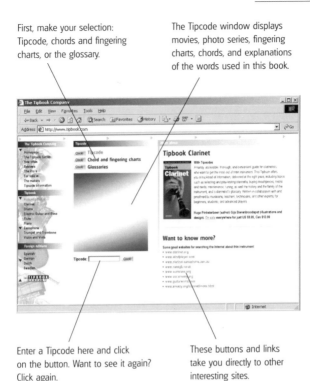

Enter a Tipcode here and click on the button. Want to see it again? Click again.

These buttons and links take you directly to other interesting sites.

Plug-ins

If the software you need to view the movies or photos is not yet installed on your computer, you'll automatically be told which software you need, and where you can download it. This kind of software (*plug-ins*) is free.

Still more at www.tipbook.com

You can find even more information at www.tipbook.com. For instance, you can look up words in the glossaries of all the Tipbooks published to date. For clarinetists, saxophonists, and flutists there are fingering charts, for drummers there are the rudiments, and for guitarists and pianists there are chord diagrams. Also included are links to some of the websites mentioned in the *Want to Know More?* section of each Tipbook.

1. A CLARINETIST?

As a clarinetist you can play in all kinds of groups and orchestras, and in many different styles, from classical music to all kinds of folk music and jazz, and much more. A chapter about everything you can do with a clarinet, about the sound of the instrument, and about larger and smaller clarinets.

With a clarinet you can play as soft as a whisper, but also loudly enough, as a soloist, to be heard above an entire orchestra. This is just one of the things that make the clarinet such a special instrument. Another is that a clarinet can sound very low, but also very high. And that you can make it sound both shy or timid and edgy or brash, or anything in between.

Violins, trumpets, and clarinets
You hear clarinetists in so many different styles because clarinets blend so well with all kinds of instruments. A clarinet sounds great with the violins in a symphony orchestra, as well as with the trumpets in a concert band, or with many other clarinets in a clarinet choir.

Wind quintets and jazz bands
Clarinets sound excellent in combination with just a piano or a human voice too, or as part of a wind quintet (clarinet, oboe, flute, bassoon, and French horn) or a jazz group. Pretty much all Dixieland jazz bands have a clarinetist, and some modern jazz groups do too. In Chapter 15 you'll find more about different kinds of groups and orchestras you can join as a clarinetist.

How you sound

For classical music, clarinetists usually want their instruments to sound dark, warm, and focused. Clarinetists who play outdoors usually want a louder, 'bigger' tone. And jazz players are often looking for a brighter, more flexible sound. All are possible, and you can largely determine the tone of the instrument yourself: How a clarinet sounds has a lot to do with how you play it.

Learning to play

Learning to play the clarinet is not too hard – to start with, anyway. With a little talent and half an hour's practice a day you'll be able to play a few standard tunes within only two or three months. What takes much longer is learning to make the instrument sound as beautiful as it can, because you make that sound yourself. As a clarinetist it's also up to you to make sure that you play in tune – just like violinists, say.

A wide variety

Clarinets come in many different variations. They can be made of wood or plastic; most are nearly black but they're also available in bright colors; and they come with all kinds of different mechanisms. All of those differences are discussed in this book.

A B-flat clarinet and a bass clarinet.

Large and small

Besides the 'regular' clarinet there are many other types – the large bass clarinet, for example, shown in the drawing above. It's is a good deal bigger, which makes it sound much lower. Playing the bass clarinet is not quite the same as simply playing a big clarinet – which is why some clarinetists specialize in that instrument. There are even larger clarinets too, and much smaller ones. You will find them in Chapter 11.

B-flat clarinet

To distinguish the 'regular' clarinet from the smaller and larger clarinets it is referred to as *soprano clarinet in B-flat* (♭), *B-flat soprano*, or simply *B-flat clarinet*. These terms will be explained in the following chapters.

2. A QUICK TOUR

With all of those keys and rods, a clarinet looks more complicated than it really is. In this chapter you will see which parts make up a clarinet and what all those components are for, and you'll read more about some of the other clarinets.

Essentially, a clarinet is a long tube with holes in it. Just as on a recorder, you play the lowest note by closing off all of those *toneholes*. If you open the last hole, the tone goes up. If you then open the next tonehole, the tone goes up some more, and so on.

Finger extensions

The toneholes of a clarinet are too far apart for you to be able to cover them all with your fingers. Besides, there are more toneholes than you have fingers. That's why the instrument has *keys*, which act as extensions to your fingers.

Five sections

A clarinet consists of five main sections. Right at the top is the *mouthpiece* with the *reed*, which is held in place by the *ligature*. When you play the clarinet, you make the reed vibrate. The reed in turn makes the air in the clarinet vibrate – and vibrating air is sound.

Barrel

Under the mouthpiece is the *barrel*, which indeed resembles a barrel. You use it to tune the clarinet, so it's also known as the *tuning barrel*.

Upper joint and lower joint

The two largest sections of the clarinet are the *upper joint* or *left-hand joint*, which you hold with your left hand when you play, and the *lower* or *right-hand joint*.

Thumb rest

The weight of the clarinet rests on your right thumb. On many clarinets, the *thumb rest* can be set a little bit higher or lower, to adjust it to your hands and your technique.

The bell

At the bottom of the lower joint is the *bell*, the widely flaring end of the clarinet.

MECHANISM

The keys and *key rods* or *axles* are collectively called the *mechanism* or the *keywork*. It looks rather complicated, but it isn't really.

Your fingers   Tipcode CLR-001

The mechanism becomes a lot easier to understand if you only look at the keys and levers on which you actually put your fingers. They're clearly shown in the illustration on the opposite page.

Six rings

Clarinets usually have six *ring keys* or *rings*, five of them at the front of the instrument. The sixth is at the back, by your left thumb.

Seventeen keys

Most clarinets have seventeen

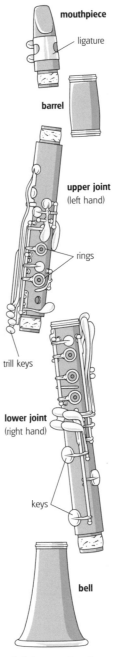

mouthpiece

ligature

barrel

upper joint
(left hand)

rings

trill keys

lower joint
(right hand)

keys

bell

A clarinet consists of
five sections.

5

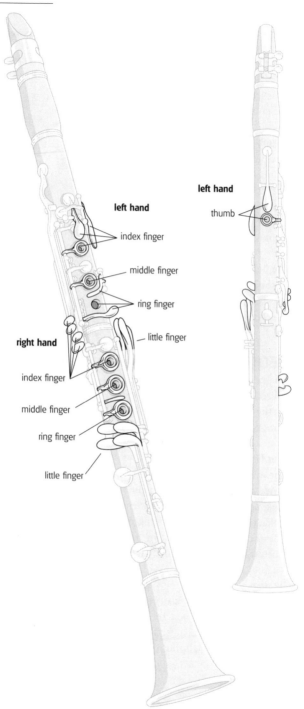

left hand

index finger

middle finger

ring finger

little finger

right hand

index finger

middle finger

ring finger

little finger

left hand

thumb

keys, in addition to those six rings. These instruments are usually described as *17/6*. Some clarinets come with extra keys or rings.

Closed keys

If you have a clarinet handy, you can see that most of the keys are closed, when you are not playing. The small keys at the top, for instance. There are springs that make sure they close again after you have opened them.

Open keys

There are only four keys that are open when you are not playing. One is right at the end of the clarinet. When you close that key along with all the others, you play the very lowest note, the low E.

Double names

You can use that lowest key to play not just the low E, but also a much higher-sounding B. For that reason, this key is called the *E/B key*. Most of the other keys and rings are also used for at least two different notes, so they all have double names too.

Fingering charts

Fingering charts show you exactly which keys and toneholes you must close to play a particular note.

THE REGISTERS

On the back of the clarinet is a special key, which you operate with your left thumb. Without this *register key* you can play only a limited number of notes on a clarinet.

Higher register   Tipcode CLR-002

If you open the register key by pressing it with your left thumb, you are suddenly able to play a whole series of new, higher-sounding notes. In other words, pressing the register key makes you enter a higher *register*.

A fingering chart showing a low B-flat fingering.

7

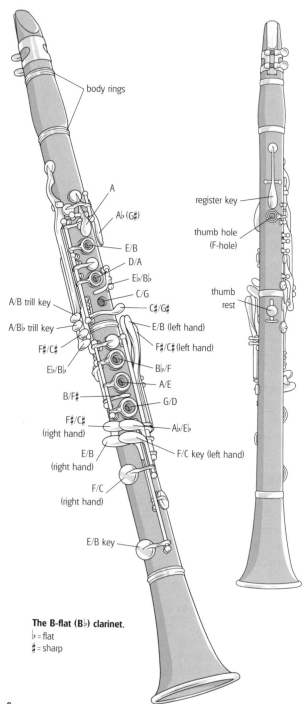

body rings

A

A♭ (G♯)

E/B

D/A

E♭/B♭

C/G

A/B trill key

C♯/G♯

A/B♭ trill key

E/B (left hand)

F♯/C♯

F♯/C♯ (left hand)

E♭/B♭

B♭/F

A/E

B/F♯

G/D

F♯/C♯
(right hand)

A♭/E♭

E/B
(right hand)

F/C key (left hand)

F/C
(right hand)

E/B key

register key

thumb hole
(F-hole)

thumb
rest

The B-flat (B♭) clarinet.
♭ = flat
♯ = sharp

Chalumeau register

When the register key is closed, you are playing the notes of the bottom register. This is also known as the *chalumeau register*.

Clarinet register

And with the register key open, you can play all the notes of the higher-sounding *clarinet register* – also known as *clarion*, *clarino*, or *upper register*.

E and B

When you keep all the keys closed, you are playing the lowest note of the chalumeau register (the low E). If you then open just the register key, you hear the lowest note of the clarinet register (the B), which sounds a lot higher.

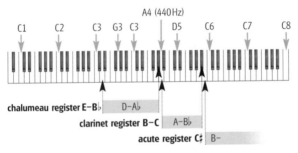

The B♭ clarinet has three registers (displayed in concert pitch).

Twelfth

On the piano keyboard above you can see that those two notes span twelve white keys. This tonal distance is called a *twelfth*.

Other names

That's why the register key is sometimes called the *12th key*: It makes everything sound a twelfth higher. Some clarinetists call it the *speaker key* instead, or – incorrectly – the *octave key* (see page 110–112).

Higher still

On the clarinet you can play even higher than the clarinet register. This highest register is usually called the *altissimo* or *acute register*. It can easily take you a couple of years before you learn to play those high notes.

Modes

The registers are also referred to as *modes*: the low (chalumeau), middle (clarinet), and high (altissimo) modes.

MORE ABOUT KEYS

Keys get all kinds of different names too. For instance, some clarinetists refer to the E/B key as the E key, while others call it the B key.

Numbers

The keys are sometimes numbered instead. Unfortunately, not everyone does it the same way. What one book calls key 5b may be key 12 in another. So that can be confusing.

Twice the same

Most clarinets have three keys that you can operate with either your left little finger or your right little finger. They are the keys E/B, F/C, and F-sharp/C-sharp (F♯/C♯). This explains why those key names are shown twice on the illustration on page 8. Which little finger you use for the note will depend mostly on the notes you play just before or just after it.

Trill keys

Your little fingers and index fingers control more than one key each. Your right index finger has no fewer than five keys to operate: one ring key, and the four keys that you press with the side of your finger. Although these side keys are commonly known as *trill keys*, only the upper two are specifically used for playing trills.

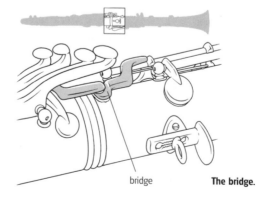

bridge   **The bridge.**

Bridge

Under the trill keys you can see the *bridge*. As it connects the rings of the lower joint with the second ring of the upper joint, this mechanism is also known as the *connection* or the *correspondence*.

Pads

Inside every *key cup* is a *pad*. This is a small disc covered with a soft material that ensures that the key seals the tonehole properly, just as your fingertip would: noiseless and without air leaking out. Key cups are also known as *pad cups*.

IN B-FLAT

The most commonly used clarinet is the B-flat clarinet. If you play a C on this clarinet, you hear a B-flat, which is exactly one whole note lower than a C. Why is that?

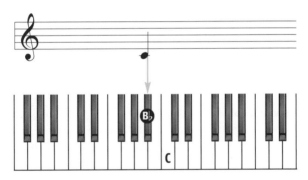

On a B♭ clarinet, a written C sounds the same pitch as a B♭ on the piano.

Playing fingerings

If your chart shows a C, on a *ledger line* under the staff, you close the three toneholes by your left hand. You are then playing a C *fingering*. On a B-flat that fingering will sound a B-flat.

C clarinets

Some clarinets are pitched in C instead. If you play a C fingering on one, you'll hear a C. That seems simpler, but there is one problem: Being pitched a little higher, a C clarinet is slightly shorter than a B-flat clarinet. The extra length of a B-flat instrument makes it sound just a little warmer, fuller, and darker. That's why just about everyone prefers to play it.

E-flat and A

In many orchestras you will also find the small E-flat clarinet. This sounds a good deal higher and brighter than the B-flat clarinet. Clarinetists in symphony orchestras often use an A clarinet as well as the B-flat clarinet. Being slightly longer, the A instrument sounds a little lower and darker. All other clarinets are listed in Chapter 11.

Transposing instruments

Instruments not pitched in C – are called *transposing instruments*. The composer writes *transposed parts* for them.

Write a C, hear E-flat

If a composer wants to use the bright sound of an E-flat clarinet, there'll have to be a special chart for that clarinet. If the tone E-flat needs to sound, that chart will show the note C. You finger this C, and the audience hears an E-flat. That's all there is to it.

Concert B-flat

Some alternative names: If you finger a C on a B-flat clarinet, you'll hear a B-flat, which is also known as *concert B-flat* or *B-flat concert pitch*.

Soprano clarinets

The clarinets mentioned above are known as soprano clarinets. Sopranino clarinets sound higher; alto and bass clarinets sound lower.

ALTO AND BASS CLARINETS

Alto and bass clarinets are very popular instruments. At first sight the bass looks very different from the soprano, even moreso than the alto. It is a whole lot bigger, and to to avoid it becoming too long to handle, it has a curved, metal neck, and a metal bow connecting the bell to the instrument.

Closed hole keys

Bass clarinets don't have ring keys or open toneholes, since most of their toneholes are too big to cover with your fingers. Instead, they have *closed-hole keys*, also known as *plateau-style keys* or *covered keys*. Bass clarinets also have more keys that you can operate with your left- and right-hand little fingers. Otherwise, the mechanism is basically the same.

In B-flat

The bass clarinet is usually pitched in B-flat. It sounds exactly one octave lower (eight white keys on a piano) than a soprano B-flat clarinet, when you play the same fingerings.

Alto clarinets

The alto clarinet is somewhere between the ordinary clarinet and the bass clarinet. Some alto clarinets have both closed-hole keys and rings, others have only closed-hole keys. Alto clarinets are pitched in E-flat. Using the same fingerings, it sounds a *fifth* (five white keys on a piano) lower than a soprano B-flat clarinet. All the other clarinets are described in Chapter 11, *The Family.*

The alto clarinet: bigger than a B♭ clarinet and smaller than a bass clarinet.

HOW HIGH AND HOW LOW

Clarinets can sound very low, but also very high: They have a large *range*. Between the highest and the lowest note is a difference of more than three and a half octaves. The range of a bass clarinet is even bigger: A good player can span more than four octaves.

Seeing and hearing   Tipcode CLR-004

On the piano keyboard below you can see how big the

ranges of the small E-flat, the B-flat, the alto, and the bass clarinet are, and by using the Tipcode above you can hear them too.

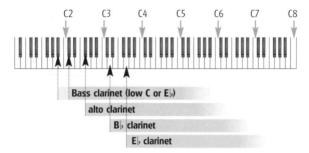

The (sounding) ranges of the four most popular clarinets.

Several E notes

When all the keys of the regular B-flat clarinet are closed, you play the E. This is not the only E you can play on a clarinet: You can also play this note one and two octaves higher.

E3-E6

Notes are numbered to identify the octave in which they are played. The lowest E on the clarinet is E3, the highest is E6. Alternatively, you may find indications such as an underscore e (for E3) and e''' (e, three-lined octave; equals E6).

French and German

This Tipbook is mainly about the *French clarinet* or *Boehm clarinet*. There are also *German clarinets*, which sound and look different. They are mainly used in Germany, but you may come across them elsewhere. There's more about them on page 48 and onwards.

are more expensive, but can be tailored exactly to
eds.

es

may want to check whether there are any teacher
es or music schools in your vicinity. These
s may offer extras such as ensemble playing,
sses, and clinics, in a wide variety of styles, and
levels.

questions

st visit to a teacher, don't simply ask how much
re are some other questions.
oductory lesson included? This is a good way
how well you get on with the teacher, and, for
, with the instrument.
er interested in taking you on as a student if
doing it **for the fun of it**, or are you expected
t least three hours a day?
e to make a large investment in method
away, or is **course material provided**?
rd your lessons, so that you can listen at home
ound, and once more to what's been said?
wed to fully concentrate on **the style of
nt to play**, or will you be required to learn
Or will you be stimulated to do so?
going to make you **practice scales** for two
you be pushed onto a stage as soon as

ts mainly play classical music, many
nd to give 'classical' lessons. Of course,
equally at home in other musical styles,

ivals, concerts, and sessions. Go watch
ras, clarinet choirs, and other groups.
ys to learn to play is seeing other
Living legends or local amateurs –
ing experience. And the best way to
ot!

3. LEARNING TO PLAY

The clarinet is not the hardest instrument to learn to play, but it's not the easiest either. You can master a few basic tunes in a matter of weeks or months, but you can also spend years working on your technique and on developing a beautiful tone – just like with any other instrument.

To make a clarinet sound good, you need to learn a good breathing technique. Playing the clarinet or any other wind instrument involves more than simply blowing a lot of air into it. Only with good air stream control can you play in tune, sound great, and play long phrases too.

Embouchure

The way your instrument sounds also has a lot to do with how you use your lips, jaws, tongue and all the muscles around them, when you play. Altogether that is known as the *embouchure*.

Mechanism

It doesn't usually take too long to get used to the complex-looking keywork of the instrument. After all, it was devised to make a clarinet player's life as easy as possible. To start with you'll play only in the lowest register. After a few months to a year you'll start using the register key, which means you'll also be playing in the clarinet register. You won't get to the very highest notes for some while longer.

Too young?

The fingers of children younger than 10 or 11 years old are

often too thin to stop the toneholes, or to reach all of the keys. What's more, their thumbs may not be strong enough to bear the weight of the instrument, which easily weighs some 1½–1¾ pounds (700–800 grams).

Solutions

A neck strap alleviates the weight problem. You can also start out on a smaller clarinet, such as the E-flat model: There are also special ones with mechanisms made for smaller hands, and even dedicated children's clarinets.

Neck strap

If you use a neck strap, the weight of the clarinet is on your neck rather than resting on your thumb only. Straps with a wide, elastic neck band are very popular. Many clarinets have an eye into which you can hook the strap. In case yours doesn't, straps often have a leather flap to attach it to the thumb rest.

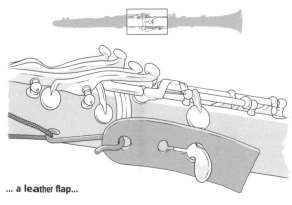

... a leather flap...

Smaller clarinet

A neck strap won't help you if your fingers are too thin or too short. Some teachers will advise you to start on a smaller clarinet, such as an E-flat clarinet, if this is a problem for you. However, there are two drawbacks: You'll later have to get used to a B-flat clarinet, because it plays slightly differently, and there are very few affordable E-flat clarinets around. One exception is the lightweight Kinder-Klari, which was designed for children. Some brands have regular clarinets on which all the rings have been replaced with plateau-style (closed-hole) keys, so that you can stop the toneholes even with very small fingers.

Even younger

The design of the British Lyons c[...] aimed at children aged from fi[...] With its plastic mechanism, this [...] looks very different. It weighs [...] third of a regular clarinet, it [...] small toneholes, all the keys [...] close together, it needs less [...] and is more durable.

Braces and baby teeth

Playing the clarinet is usua[...] if you wear braces, althoug[...] a long time in one go, a l[...] start giving you some trou[...] become difficult if you'r[...] teeth: If you don't have [...] instrument may start w[...]

LESSONS

If you take clarinet [...] about everything [...] the clarinet – [...] embouchure to pl[...] reading music to [...]

Locating a teach[...]

Looking for a p[...] may have teac[...] refer you to or[...] local Musicia[...] school in yo[...] teachers in [...] may also ch[...] magazines [...] the *Yellow* [...] charge be[...] make ho[...]

Group [...]

Instea[...] group[...]

lessons[...]
your n[...]

Collectiv[...]

You also [...] collectiv[...] collectiv[...] master cl[...] at various[...]

Questions,[...]

On your fi[...] it costs. He[...]

- Is an **intr**[...] to find ou[...] that matte[...]
- Is the teach[...] you are jus[...] to practice [...]
- Do you ha[...] books right [...]
- Can you **reco**[...] to how you s[...]
- Are you allo[...] **music you wa**[...] other styles? [...]
- Is this teacher [...] years, or will [...] possible?

Not classical

Because clarineti[...] clarinet teachers t[...] some teachers are [...] if not moreso.

Listen and play

And finally, visit fes[...] and listen to orches[...] One of the best w[...] musicians at work.[...] every concert's a lear[...] learn to play? Play a [...]

18

PRACTICING

What goes for every instrument goes especially for wind instruments: It's better to practice half an hour every day than a whole day once a week. This is especially true for your embouchure: If you don't play for a few days, you'll feel it straight away.

Three times ten

How long should you practice? That depends on your talent and on what you want to achieve. As an indication: Half an hour a day usually results in steady progress. If playing half an hour at a stretch seems too long, try dividing it up into two quarter-hour sessions, or three of ten minutes each.

In tune

Practice is also important for learning to play your instrument musically – which certainly involves playing in tune. The longer you play, and the better you learn to listen to yourself, the easier it will be to get each note perfectly in tune.

Neighbors

There are few instruments you can play as softly as a clarinet, but of course you won't always. If neighbors or housemates are bothered by your playing, it may be enough to simply agree to fixed practice times. If you really play a lot, it may be better to insulate a room. Even a very large cupboard can be big enough. There are books available on sound insulation, or you can hire a specialized contractor. Of course, it may be easier to find a place that works a little better for practicing.

On CD

Playing the clarinet is something you usually do in a group, so it's often more fun to practice 'together' too – even if there aren't any other musicians around. There are all kinds of CDs available to play along to, in all kinds of styles, for beginners as well as for more advanced clarinetists. Your own part is left off, leaving the other musicians for you to play with.

Computer lessons

If you have a computer handy, you can also use special

CD-ROMs to practice with. Some feature entire orchestras: You can decide for yourself how fast you want a piece to be played, and which parts you want to hear. There is also software that allows you to slow down difficult phrases on a recording, so you can find out what's going on at your own tempo.

Metronome

Most pieces of music are supposed to be played just as fast at the end as at the beginning. Playing with a metronome helps you to achieve this. A metronome is a small mechanical or electronic device that ticks or bleeps out a steady adjustable pulse, so you can tell immediately if you're dragging or speeding.

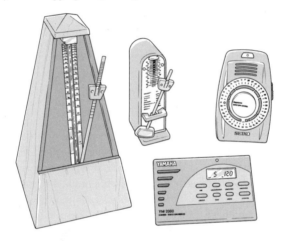

Two mechanical metronomes and two electronic ones.

Recording

If you record your clarinet lessons, you can listen to what was said, and especially how you sounded, when you get home. You can learn a lot by listening carefully to yourself playing. That's why many musicians record themselves when they are practicing. All you need is a cassette recorder with a built-in microphone. Better equipment (a minidisk player with a separate microphone, for instance) is more expensive, but the recordings are usually more enjoyable to listen to.

4. BUYING A CLARINET

You can buy a new clarinet for as little as three or four hundred dollars. The most expensive clarinets cost ten times as much, if not more. Of course you can rent one first, to find out whether the instrument suits you. Or you can buy one secondhand. In this chapter you can read what you need to know before you go out to get yourself a clarinet. All the technical details and tips for listening and play-testing are in Chapter 5, *A Good Clarinet*.

Most affordable clarinets are made of plastic. They usually come with a case and a mouthpiece, and often one or two reeds as well. Plastic clarinets cannot crack, and they weigh less and need less maintenance than wooden instruments.

Wood

From around seven or eight hundred dollars you can buy a wooden clarinet, which will usually give you a more beautiful, warmer tone. A slightly more expensive instrument may also have a better mechanism that is easier to play, lasts longer, and needs less adjustment.

Silver-plated

If you spend a bit more, you can get an instrument with a mechanism that is silver-plated instead of nickel-plated. That makes the clarinet look nicer, but it doesn't make it sound any better.

Mid-range

Intermediate clarinetists often spend one to two thousand dollars when buying a new instrument. That extra money buys you a clarinet that usually plays and sounds better, because better materials have been used and because more care has been devoted to construction. It's not always easy to tell a higher-priced instrument from its appearance – mainly because even most cheap instruments look very good.

Professional

Advanced and professional players often use instruments that cost more than two and a half or three thousand dollars. The more you spend, the harder it becomes to hear or see the differences. The most expensive clarinets cost around five to six thousand.

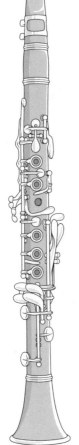

Other clarinets

Most other clarinets are more expensive, some because they're bigger, and also because fewer of them are made. As an example, you can expect to pay fifteen hundred dollars for a plastic bass clarinet, the most expensive wooden versions costing easily six or more times as much. E-flat clarinets are smaller than B-flat clarinets, but they're not really cheaper. You hardly find them in the lowest price range. The same goes for soprano clarinets in other tunings (*e.g.*, A, C or D).

THE SHOP

A clarinet is a precision instrument that needs to be properly maintained and adjusted. It also needs a full overhaul now and again. That's why you're best off buying your instrument in a shop where they do those jobs themselves. Then you know that they know what they are doing, and that they probably won't send you home with a lousy, badly adjusted instrument. Even new clarinets may need to be checked and adjusted one more time before they play well.

An E♭ clarinet.

COA

Every clarinet needs to be checked and readjusted from time to time (COA: cleaning, oiling, adjusting). If you have bought a new instrument, that service may be free the first time, or for the first year. Some shops and technicians may even send you a reminder when it's time for a COA.

Another store

When you're going to buy an instrument, it can't do any harm to visit a few different stores or clarinet workshops, because every store has its own sound, and you'll hear different stories and opinions depending on where you go. What's more, not all stores stock all the brands.

Time and space

The more clarinets there are to choose from, the harder the choice can be – on the other hand, the better your chances of finding exactly the clarinet you're looking for. Be sure to take your time, and remember that it's better to come back another time than to play one hour or more in a row. Some stores have separate rooms for play-testing, so that you don't bother the other customers – or vice versa.

On approval

In some cases you may be able to take an instrument on approval, so that you can assess it at home at your leisure. This is more common with expensive clarinets than cheap ones, and you are more likely to be given the option if you are a good clarinetist than if you are choosing your first instrument. An advantage of trying out a clarinet at home is that you are used to how your own instrument sounds there, which helps you to compare properly. In a store everything sounds different – even your own clarinet.

Not the same

Even two 'identical' clarinets will never sound exactly the same. So always buy the instrument you thought sounded best, and not an 'identical' one from the warehouse. The same goes for mouthpieces.

Another clarinetist

In order to hear the differences between one clarinet and another, you need to be able to play well, which can be a problem if you're going to buy your first instrument. So take someone with you who can play, or find stores where someone on the staff can.

Buying online

You can also buy musical instruments online or by mail-order. This makes it impossible to compare instruments, of course, but most online and mail-order companies offer a return service for most or all of their products: If you're not happy with it, you can send it back within a certain period of time. Of course the instrument should be in new condition when you send it back.

RENTING

Rather than buying one, you can rent a clarinet. Expect to pay around fifty to seventy-five dollars for a period of three months. Some shops rent them out only for longer periods. The exact rental fee, usually a percentage of the retail price of the instrument, will also depend on what it covers, *i.e.* do you rent a new or a used (rental-return) instrument, and are insurance and maintenance included? Some stores may ask for a deposit; others require your credit card number.

... and then buying

Some stores offer a rent-to-own program, where all or part of the rental fee you've been paying will be deducted if you decide to buy the instrument in the end. Alternatively, you may get a discount on a new instrument, after the rental period: The longer you've been renting, the larger the discount. These are just two of the many variations you may come across.

SECONDHAND

As little as two to three hundred dollars can get you a properly checked and adjusted secondhand clarinet that you'll be able to play for years. Of course, you can also spend much more, up to thousands of dollars. One of the advantages of a good secondhand instrument is that you'll probably be able to sell it again for a good price, provided it's been well maintained.

Privately or in a store

Secondhand clarinets are sold through music stores, or they're offered for sale in the classified sections in newspapers, on bulletin boards in stores, and on the Internet. If you buy an instrument through an ad, you may pay less than in a store. After all, the store owner needs to make a living too.

In a music store

All the same, buying from a music store does have advantages. The instrument may have been checked and adjusted, and it may come with a warranty; you can go back if you have any questions, you may be able to choose between a number of instruments, and in some cases you can even exchange the secondhand clarinet you bought for a different one within a certain period. Another advantage: A good store will never charge you much more than an instrument is worth. A private seller might, either because he doesn't know better or because he thinks you don't.

A second opinion

If you go to buy a secondhand clarinet, it's even more important to take along an advanced player who knows about the instrument – especially if you're going to buy privately. Otherwise you might turn down a decent clarinet just because it doesn't look good, or get saddled with an instrument that looks great but doesn't sound good or play in tune. Some technical tips for buying secondhand instruments begin on page 58.

Appraisal

If you want to be sure you're not paying too much, get the instrument appraised first. A good store or workshop can tell you exactly what a clarinet is worth, whether it needs any work done, and what the extra work costs.

Sieve

Many decent clarinets in disrepair can be made to sound good, even if they leak like a sieve and you can barely get a sound out of them. If you buy an instrument like this, you should be aware that it can easily cost you hundreds of dollars to get it fixed.

AND FINALLY

What you consider the best clarinet may well be the one your favorite clarinetist plays. Does that mean you should buy the same instrument? There isn't much point. Even if you use exactly the same clarinet, the same mouthpiece, and the same reed, you'll still sound different.

One on two, two on one

If you get a clarinetist to play two different clarinets, you're likely to hear little difference. But two different clarinetists on the same instrument won't sound the same at all. In other words: The sound depends more on the player than on the instrument.

The same

Even so, you often see all clarinetists in an orchestra playing the same brand of clarinet (they often have to), and even using the same type of mouthpiece. This helps the clarinet section to sound as a whole, rather than as a number of clarinetists.

Brochures

If you want to be well informed before you go out to buy or rent an instrument, get hold of as many clarinet brochures and catalogs as you can find, along with the price lists.

Magazines, books and Internet

There are also various magazines that offer reviews and other articles on the instrument. Quite a few clarinet books are available too, as well as loads of information on the Internet. You'll find titles, addresses and other information beginning on page 129.

Conventions and workshops

All kinds of get-togethers are organized for clarinetists, from clarinet conventions and courses to workshops and demonstrations. You can find out more about your instrument there, and you'll always learn something from the other clarinetists you meet (see *Want to Know More?*, page 129).

5. A GOOD CLARINET

If you lay ten soprano clarinets side by side, the differences may be hard to spot. They're all the same shape, and all the keys, rings and holes are in the same places. Yet one may cost five times more than the next, another may sound much better, and still another may play much better. This chapter tells you why, and offers tips for play-testing and evaluating the sound of clarinets.

More than anything else, how a clarinet sounds depends on you: A good clarinetist can make even a cheap instrument sound impressive. Next in importance are the reed, the mouthpiece, and the barrel; all three are discussed separately in Chapters 6 and 7.

This chapter
Why two clarinets can sound and play so differently is linked to all kinds of things. This chapter begins with the material an instrument is made of. The next subject discussed is the inside of the clarinet (the *bore*), which is one of its most important 'parts.' After that you can read more about the toneholes (page 35), the mechanism (page 38), extra keys and the full-Boehm clarinet (page 44), German clarinets (page 48), and secondhand instruments (page 58), among other subjects.

With your ears
If you prefer to select a clarinet using your ears alone, then go straight to the tips for listening and play-testing, which begin on page 54.

All the same

Clarinetists rarely agree about anything. The following chapters won't tell you who is right, or what is best, but rather what various experts think about different issues. You'll only discover who you agree with by playing and by listening – to clarinets, and to clarinetists.

All clarinets

This book is mainly about the B-flat clarinet, but most of what you read here also applies to all other clarinets. Here and there you'll find comments specifically about those 'other' instruments.

MATERIALS

The cheapest clarinets are made of plastic, the more expensive ones of wood, and in between are wooden instruments with a plastic bell and barrel. What are the differences?

Plastic: the advantages

Plastic clarinets have many advantages. They are less expensive, can't crack, need less maintenance, and weigh considerably less (about a quarter of a pound, or 100 grams) than wooden instruments. This is especially good news for children.

Playing outdoors

Plastic clarinets are also better resistant to rain, sunshine, and rapid changes in air humidity or temperature, and you don't have to keep retuning them when it gets colder or hotter. This is why they are often used in groups that play outdoors.

Preferably wood

Even so, most clarinetists prefer to play wooden instruments, as they usually sound richer, darker, and warmer. That's certainly not all because of the material: The main reason why wooden clarinets tend to sound better is simply that clarinet makers use wood to make their better instruments.

Blacker and shinier

Most plastic clarinets are easy to recognize: They look 'blacker' and shinier than wooden ones. Some makers use plastics that look a little like wood (*i.e., wood-grained polymers*), or they make the surface of their plastic instruments matte, or a little less smooth (*brushed*). Others also make colored clarinets, in bright yellow, red, blue, or other colors.

Attractive names

Because 'plastic' has a cheap sound to it, most manufacturers come up with a more attractive name for the material they use, such as Resotone, Resonite, Sonority Resin, or Grena 2000. Plastic clarinets are also referred to as *composition* or *synthetic* clarinets.

Only the barrel and the bell

Some otherwise wooden clarinets have a plastic barrel and bell. This helps to keep the price down, especially in the case of the bell: To make a wooden bell, you need a fair-sized chunk of expensive wood. The sound of the instrument will often audibly improve if you replace the plastic barrel with a wooden one. As a rule, replacing the bell will have less effect.

Wooden clarinets

Most wooden clarinets are made of an African wood variety that is extremely hard, heavy, and very dark – indeed, almost black in color. It is usually called grenadilla, although you may come across other names, such as African blackwood, m'pingo, and ebony, or the official name, *Dalbergia melanoxylon*. The French brand Buffet also makes clarinets from a mixture of (mainly) resin and compressed grenadilla powder.

Other kinds of wood

Less common, but sometimes also used for clarinets is West Indian ebony, which is also known as *Brya ebenus*, cocuswood, or granadilla. Rosewood, a reddish-brown wood that is said to give a lighter, softer or sweeter tone, is rarer still.

Breaking it in

In order to prevent a new wooden clarinet from cracking, it's best to break it in carefully. That way the wood, which has been dried in the factory, gets used to the moisture you blow into the instrument. One approach would be to play

it for fifteen minutes every day for the first week, and fifteen minutes per day longer every following week. Or you could start with five minutes the first day, and add five more every day; or play half an hour a day for the first month, or ...

Color

Some brands give all their clarinets an extra dark hue by staining them. Other brands don't color them, and some brands offer staining as an option. There is no audible difference.

Metal parts

Large clarinets, such as the alto and the bass, have metal *necks* instead of barrels. The bell is just about always made of metal too, as is the bow that joins it to the instrument.

Metal clarinets

In Turkish, Greek, and other international folk music groups, you may find soprano clarinets made entirely of metal. You'd expect them to sound very different from wooden or plastic clarinets, but in fact the difference is barely audible. Metal clarinets are a lot lighter, because their walls are very thin. Single-walled metal clarinets look very thin too.

Larger clarinets – such as this bass clarinet, which extends to low C – have metal necks, bows, and bells.

THE BORE

Many brochures state the width of the inside of the tube for each clarinet, known as the *bore*. The dimensions of the bore have a major effect on how an instrument sounds and plays.

Wide or narrow

Most clarinets have a bore of between 0.577" and 0.585" (14.65–14.85 mm), measured halfway up the instrument. When you are playing, these small differences seem much bigger than they do on paper.

Wide

Clarinets with a really wide bore (up to 0.591"/15 mm) are mostly used by beginners, because they respond more easily. Jazz clarinetists are also likely to chose this type of bore: Though it requires more air, it gives you the volume you often need for playing jazz, and a sound that is usually described as big and open.

Narrow

For a darker, warmer and more subdued 'classical' sound, you'll probably choose an instrument with a narrower bore and a greater blowing resistance.

Different country, different bore

Which bore is most popular varies from country to country. Clarinetists in France usually go for a narrow bore; in Austria they prefer a wide bore, and most US clarinetists play something in between. German clarinets come with both narrow and wide bores.

Inches to millimeters

Bore sizes are often given only in inches. To convert to millimeters, multiply that size by 25.4. So for example, a 0.575" bore is 0.575 x 25.4 = 14.60 mm.

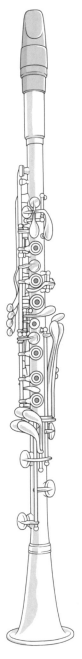

A single-walled metal clarinet.

Cylindrical

The tube of a clarinet is the same width along the greater part of its length: Clarinets have a largely *cylindrical* bore. At certain points, though, the bore becomes narrower, or wider.

Air column

The exact shape of the bore is very important for how a clarinet plays and sounds. Why? When you blow, the reed makes the air in the clarinet vibrate, and vibrating air is sound. In other words, this vibrating air column 'makes' the sound of the clarinet. The character of a clarinet's sound depends to a very large extent on the shape of the air column – and that shape is of course the same as the shape of the bore.

Conical

Towards the end the bore becomes steadily wider. This *conical* section usually begins somewhere about halfway down the lower joint, and is of course most pronounced at the bell.

Reverse cone

At the top of the upper joint of the clarinet, the tube usually narrows by an almost invisible amount (*reverse cone* or *reversing cone*). This produces some extra resistance, and it makes the sound a little darker, warmer, deeper, and more colorful. A clarinet with an upper joint that doesn't get narrower, or does so only by a very small amount, usually blows very easily, having a rather bright, open sound – just like an instrument with a wide bore. You'll get a warmer, more focused sound when using an instrument with a tapered bore.

All kinds of names

Because this narrowing at the top is so important, all kinds of words are

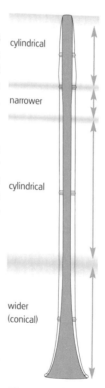

cylindrical

narrower

cylindrical

wider
(conical)

The shape of the air column is important for the character of the sound.

used in brochures and books to describe that small section of the bore. For instance, a *linear cone* means that the tube becomes wider evenly, and *dual taper* means it does so in two steps (first a little more quickly, then a little more gradually, or the other way around). Many instruments have a *polycylindrical* or a *polyconical bore*: a bore that narrows in three or more steps.

More, better, richer
All of that jargon is only really important to clarinet makers, and not to players. After all, you don't buy a clarinet because it has a particular bore but because of the way it plays and sounds. Of course, brochures do tell you lots about the advantages of the bores they use, from more volume to a tone that is easier to control or a richer sound.

Smooth
If you look through the lower joint and upper joint of your clarinet, you can see how smoothly the bore is finished. A smooth bore allows an instrument to sound easier and 'smoother'. If a secondhand clarinet has a messy-looking bore, that may be because it hasn't been kept clean properly.

Wall thickness
Some clarinets have thicker walls than others. A thicker wall is said to give a 'thicker,' more robust sound that carries further (*projection*). An instrument with a thin wall usually responds better and sounds lighter, sweeter, and less penetrating.

Big clarinets
Naturally enough, bigger clarinets have bigger bores. To give you an idea: Alto clarinets usually have a bore of between 0.670" and 0.710" (17–18 mm), bass clarinets between 0.905" and 0.945" (23–24 mm) and E-flat clarinets somewhere around 0.530" (13.5 mm).

THE BELL
The bell is more important to the sound than you might think. It doesn't just influence the sound of the *long-tube notes*, which you play with all or almost all of the

toneholes closed, but also the notes that sound from the middle section of the clarinet. Without the bell, your instrument sounds much less resonant than it does with the bell attached.

Try it out

It follows that a clarinet may sound slightly different with one bell than with another. A bell with a wider flare can open up the sound a little, for instance, and a bell with a slightly thicker wall can make for a slightly 'thicker,' darker sound. To be able to hear those differences you need to be a competent musician and have a good instrument. If so, it can really be worthwhile to experiment with different bells.

Position

Some clarinetists with very good ears even carefully rotate the bell until they've found the position in which it makes the instrument sound its very best. Once that position is decided, they always fit the bell in exactly that way.

For sale separately

Bells are sold separately, not only to improve the sound of the instrument, but also to replace broken bells. Standard replacement bells soon cost around fifty dollars or more. Special bells can be a lot more expensive; there are wooden bells for bass clarinets with a thousand dollar price tag...

Bell ring

Because thin wooden bells are especially vulnerable, they usually have metal *bell rings*. Plastic clarinets have bell rings only for show, and some brands give you the choice between an instrument with a ring or without. A bell ring makes the instrument a tiny bit heavier. On wooden instruments especially, rings can come loose and thus cause buzzes.

No scratch protection

The bell ring almost never extends so far as to completely protect the wooden edge of the bell. That means that if you set down your clarinet on the bell, it won't be protected against scratches. If you use a clarinet stand, it will be (see page 94). Otherwise, it's better to lay the instrument down, with its keys pointing upwards.

BODY RINGS AND TENON RINGS

Most clarinets have metal *body rings* wherever two joints meet. These rings, also known as *joint rings* or *ferrules*, are said to make the sound a tiny bit darker. This is why some clarinets have only very thin body rings or none at all – a difference that is easier to see than to hear.

Tenon rings

The cork-covered ends of the upper and lower joints are the *tenons*. They are often reinforced with metal *tenon rings*. On cheaper clarinets, not every tenon has a ring.

A tenon without, and one with a tenon ring.

Too thick

Always check how easily the barrel, lower joint, upper joint, and bell fit together, and make sure to apply a little cork grease before you do. If the sections slide too easily, there's a chance that air will leak. If they're very hard to assemble, the tenon(s) may need to have a bit of the cork removed. A tip: Assembling a new clarinet will always be a little harder, the tenons being on the thick side. This will gradually improve with use.

TONEHOLES

Clarinets have three kinds of toneholes: Some have closed keys, others have ring keys, and a few are just open holes. The toneholes that have closed keys are slightly recessed (countersunk) and have beveled edges, which helps the pads to seal the holes properly.

Rings

The toneholes with rings have a small 'chimney,' around which the ring falls. On some clarinets these toneholes

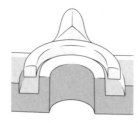

The ring falls around the chimney.

have plastic or hard rubber inserts that are often said to give a brighter sound and be less likely to crack or deform. Other instruments have *integral toneholes*, meaning that the toneholes and the joint they're in are one and the same piece of wood (see page 113–114, *How They're Made*).

Raised tonehole

The tonehole under the left ring finger really is just a hole, without a ring or a key. On some clarinets this tonehole is raised, bringing its edge up to the same level as the rings so that all of your fingers go down the same distance.

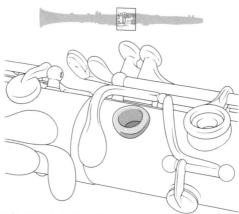

A raised D/A tonehole (Selmer).

Register tube

If you look through the upper joint of a clarinet, you will see two small metal tubes or sleeves: the *register tube* or *speaker tube* inside the register key's tonehole, and another tube inside the thumbhole. These tubes stop the moisture you blow into your clarinet from running out through those holes. They also affect the sound of an instrument and its *intonation* – how well in tune it is. That's why German clarinets have a register tube too, even though the corresponding tonehole is positioned at the top of the tube, where it can't get waterlogged.

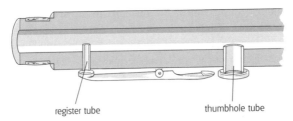

register tube   thumbhole tube

The long, narrow register tube and the shorter tube in the thumbhole.

Undercut

Most clarinets have *undercut toneholes*, which means every tonehole gets slightly wider at the bottom. Undercut toneholes may improve an instrument's tone, its response, its intonation, and much more: It makes it sound and play better, in other words. If your instrument has straight toneholes – you only really find them on cheap clarinets – it's harder to adjust the exact pitch of your notes. This actually makes things easier for beginners, since it helps to prevent pitch fluctuations.

Vent holes

Some clarinets have extra holes to make particular notes sound better or more in tune. These *resonance holes* or *vent holes* may be open, or they may have keys (see page 45).

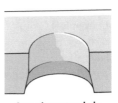

An undercut tonehole

Tuning
Tipcode CLR-005

Most orchestras, ensembles, and other groups tune to *concert A* (A4; see page 9). If you play this A on a piano, the strings vibrate 440 times per second, usually indicated as A=440 (hertz or Hz).

Or a little higher
Tipcode CLR-006

Some ensembles tune a fraction higher, for instance to A=442. That ever-so-slight adjustment makes instruments sound just a little brighter or more brilliant.

Different tunings

Ideally, your clarinet must be built to the tuning of the orchestra. For this reason, most quality clarinets come in both 440Hz and 442Hz versions, and some even in a 444Hz tuning. For each tuning, the toneholes are distributed along the clarinet slightly differently. If you do occasionally need to make your instrument sound higher or lower, you can use a longer or shorter barrel (see pages 70–72).

THE MECHANISM

The mechanism should feel nice and smooth under your fingers, and it shouldn't rattle or produce other unwanted noises. A play-testing tip: If you 'play' the instrument without blowing, it's easy to tell whether the keywork is quiet enough. Use all the keys, and pay special attention to the ones you operate with your left little finger.

A proper seal

The mechanism must ensure that all the keys close properly. If a key doesn't seal the tonehole, you won't be able to play that note – and possibly lots of others – properly, if at all. Usually this is a matter of adjustment, but a leaking key can also be caused by a torn pad (see page 47), for instance.

An even feel

Each key has a spring, which makes sure the key opens again after you've closed it, or the other way around. Some keys use *needle springs*, which do indeed look like needles. The trill keys, the A key, and the register key (the *see-saw* keys), have *leaf springs*, which are narrow metal strips. On a well-adjusted instrument, the springs are set to give all keys the same resistance.

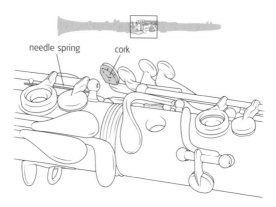

needle spring   cork

The springs must be adjusted to make all the keys feel the same.

Smooth

Keys should move smoothly. If their springs are adjusted too lightly, however, you may find that you can't really feel what you're doing, or that the keys become sluggish and don't return as quickly as they should. If a spring is much too lightly adjusted you may even blow the key open when you play real loud.

Rings

If the rings are too high when open, it's hard to seal the toneholes with your fingers. If they are too low, the coupled keys won't respond immediately as they should. Some clarinetists like their ring keys to have a fairly high adjustment, others prefer them set quite low.

Fit properly

Some clarinets appear to be built for large hands, others for small hands, or for thick fingers or thin ones. You probably won't notice such differences fully until you take the time to play the instrument. The position and shape of the left little finger levers in particular can vary. A tip: Some brands have low-budget clarinets with mechanisms made especially for children's hands.

Adjustable thumb rest

An adjustable thumb rest can make the instrument more comfortable to play. Some clarinets have an adjustment bolt that you can undo and tighten with a coin, if you don't have a screwdriver on you. A fixed thumb rest can

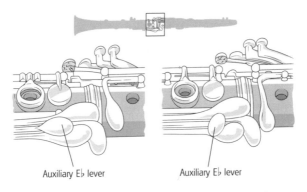

Auxiliary E♭ lever   Auxiliary E♭ lever

The differences are often greatest at the left little finger levers. In particular, look at the (auxiliary) E-flat lever.

easily be replaced with an adjustable one. If the thumb rest cuts into your thumb, buy a rubber *thumb saver*, which slides over the thumb rest.

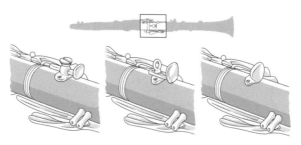

A thumb rest that you can adjust with a coin, an adjustable one with an eye to attach a neck strap to, and a simple, fixed thumb rest.

Special thumb rests

When you play, the entire weight of the clarinet rests on the furthest joint of your thumb. Especially when playing for long stretches at a time, that can cause pain and other symptoms. To avoid this, there are special thumb rests that divert the weight of the clarinet to the first joint. You can have one custom made, but you can also buy them off the shelf.

Adjustable thumb rest designed to prevent pain and other symptoms (Ton Kooiman Etude).

Neck strap

Another way to reduce the pressure on the thumb is to use a neck strap (see page 16). Although typically used by children, these are increasingly popular with adult clarinetists.

Nickel or silver

On clarinets costing up to around eight hundred to a thousand dollars, the keywork is usually nickel-plated, while on more expensive instruments it is almost always silver-plated. Sometimes you can choose – if so, the silver-plated mechanism will often cost around fifty to hundred fifty dollars extra.

The differences

The difference between nickel and silver-plating is clearly visible: Nickel has a slightly 'harder' shine than silver, and silver looks a bit whiter. Nickel is cheaper, it needs less polishing, and is more resilient than silver. On the other hand, nickel feels more slippery, which can be a problem if you tend to have sweaty fingers. What's more, some people suffer from an allergy to nickel.

Gold

If you have very acidic perspiration, it can make silver tarnish so quickly that you're better off with a nickel-plated mechanism. Or you could have your keywork gold-plated instead, which is less expensive than it sounds. New clarinets with a fully or partly gold-plated mechanism are rare. On some models only the *posts* are gold-plated, for instance.

Posts

The posts are the small pillars that attach the keywork to the clarinet. Often, some of the posts are *anchored*: A small screw stops them from twisting out of position due to the pressure of the needle springs.

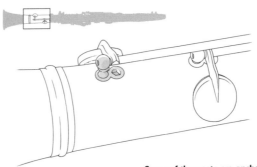

Some of the posts are anchored.

Rounded or pointed keys

Virtually all clarinets have so-called *French-style keys*, indicating that the key cups are attached by a pointed arm. The key cups come in two varieties: *rounded* (also called *rond-bombé*) or in a slightly pointed shape (*conical* or *China cup*). Virtually every clarinet has *power-forged* keys, meaning that they are shaped by pressure, when the metal is cold, rather than cast.

Trill keys

The trill keys come in two types. *Offset trill keys* have a kink just before the key cup; *in-line trill keys* don't. The movement of the key cup is a little more logical with the in-line system – it moves vertically up and down, rather than slightly diagonally. The difference isn't very meaningful, though, and you find both systems on both cheap and expensive instruments.

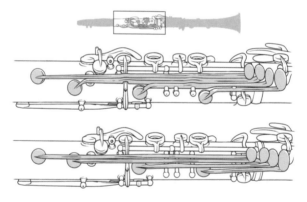

Offset (above) and in-line trill keys.

Separate mountings

What does make a difference is whether certain keys are individually mounted, having separate post mountings. If so, they tend to be easier to adjust, and the keywork may last longer. On most more expensive clarinets, each trill key is individually mounted, while on cheaper instruments the B-flat and B-keys share their posts. Some cheaper clarinets also have only three posts by the A and A-flat keys, instead of four. More expensive clarinets may have more individually mounted keys, *e.g.*, the C-sharp/G-sharp and the A-flat/E-flat keys.

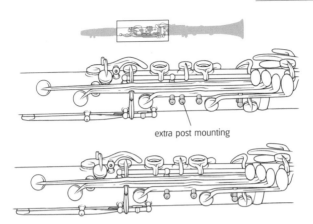

extra post mounting

An individually-mounted A♭/E♭ key (above), and a regular one.

Adjustment screws

Pretty much all clarinets have an adjustment screw on the A and A-flat keys, on the upper part of the left-hand joint.

You'll find other adjustment screws only on more expensive clarinets. Typically, the F-sharp/C-sharp and E/B keys will be adjustable, with two extra screws under the *crow foot* by your right little finger. Very occasionally, the F/C key will also have an adjustment screw, or the bridge will. Of course, a clarinet can also be adjusted without screws, but only with some very careful bending. A job for a professional, in other words.

crow foot

The adjustment screws for the F♯/C♯ and the E/B keys are in the crow foot, by the right little finger.

Cork

Some keys need to be adjusted by sticking pieces of cork of varying thickness under them – a job that is better left to a specialist. Corks are also used to make the mechanism quieter, by keeping parts from clattering against each other.

Large clarinets and German clarinets

Bass and alto clarinets and other larger instruments, with

much longer key rods, usually have more adjustment screws. Clarinets with German mechanisms often have a whole bunch too.

EXTRA KEYS

The majority of Boehm clarinets have a regular mechanism – seventeen keys and six rings (17/6) – but they're available with extra keys and other special features as well.

Auxiliary E-flat lever

Quite a few clarinets in the higher price ranges have four levers by the left little finger, instead of the usual three. That extra fourth lever, the *auxiliary E-flat lever*, is for the A-flat/E-flat key, which you can normally operate only with your right little finger. Some more expensive clarinets have this auxiliary lever as a standard. If you don't use it, you can have it removed. On other models the *auxiliary E-flat/A-flat*, as it is also known, is an option – often with a price tag of a hundred to more than two hundred dollars.

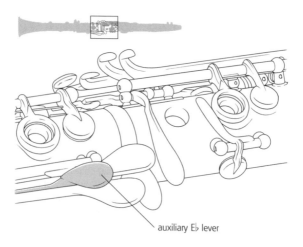

auxiliary E♭ lever

The auxiliary E♭ lever: the fourth lever by your the little finger.

Fork B-flat

With the addition of a seventh ring key, by your right index finger, you can play a B-flat by using your left ring finger and index finger. This *forked fingering* is called a *fork B-flat*. That seventh ring also makes certain trills easier.

Articulated G-sharp

Even rarer than the fork B-flat is the *articulated G-sharp* or *F-sharp/G-sharp trill key*. You can identify an articulated G-sharp by the extra closed-hole key under the G-sharp lever, and there is an extra lever on the lower joint. This system makes various trills on G-sharp or C-sharp a lot easier by allowing you to play them with your right index finger instead of your – weaker – left little finger.

Low E-flat

A clarinet with a low E-flat is just a little longer than a regular B-flat soprano. You play the extra low note with a fifth key by your right little finger.

Why not standard?

A clarinet with all the above extras is known as a *full-Boehm* instrument. Only very few manufacturers still make them. How come? Because all the additions make the instrument a lot heavier and the tone less bright, the articulated G-sharp is a complicated affair, and the seventh ring makes some trills easier but others impossible. So the regular 17/6 remains the most popular instrument, and there's hardly anything you can't play on it.

Low E vent key

Other additions are available too. For example, the occasional clarinet has a so-called *low E vent key*. If you play a low E or F, a key opens an extra tonehole at the end of the lower joint, or in the bell. This slightly

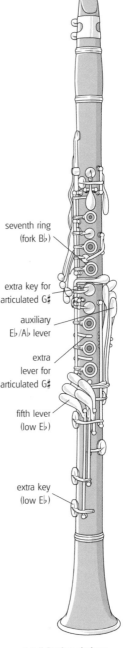

seventh ring (fork B♭)

extra key for articulated G♯

auxiliary E♭/A♭ lever

extra lever for articulated G♯

fifth lever (low E♭)

extra key (low E♭)

A full-Boehm clarinet.

raises those two notes, which often sound a little too low, and especially so on German clarinets – which is why low E vent keys are much more common on German instruments.

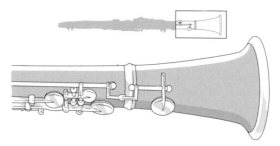

An extra key for the low E and F on the bell of a German clarinet.

Improved B-flat

The B-flat of the chalumeau register is the hardest note for clarinet makers, as it uses the same tonehole as the register key . In order to make that B-flat sound really good, the tonehole would actually need to be a bit bigger and a bit lower – but then it would be too big and too low to serve as the tonehole for the register key.

Extra key

German system clarinets often have an extra key to make the B-flat sound a little clearer. Many solutions have been provided to improve its pitch on French clarinets too, such

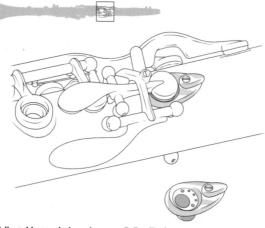

Adjustable tonehole to improve B-flat (Tutz).

as a replacement for the A-tonehole, which can be bought separately. This device can be adjusted to produce the desired pitch for B-flat.

Bass clarinet to low C

Bass clarinets always have a low E-flat, and many even go down to a low D or C. How you play those lowest notes depends on the brand, and sometimes even on the model. On some bass clarinets, you operate three keys with your right thumb and five with your little finger; on others you'll play two with your thumb and six with your little finger… A bass clarinet that goes down to the low C can easily cost a thousand dollars more than an identical instrument with E-flat as its lowest note.

Second register key

In order to improve response and intonation, some larger clarinets have two register keys. Which of the two keys opens depends on the note you are playing. For some notes in the highest register, bass clarinets also have a small extra hole in the key cup under your left index finger: To play those notes you close the key, leaving the extra hole open.

PADS

To ensure that the keys seal the toneholes properly, they are fitted with pads. Usually a pad consists of a layer of felt covered with a very thin, vulnerable membrane. This membrane is often referred to as *fish skin*, but it actually comes from cows' intestines. Most pads have two or even three layers.

Plastic

Plastic pads are becoming more and more common on clarinets. They are not affected by moisture or dryness as much as traditional pads, and they last longer. Of course you do pay a little more for them. One well-known brand name is Gore-Tex.

Cork

The keys at the bottom of the tube may have cork pads, because they are the most likely to become waterlogged by the moisture that collects in the instrument. Some players prefer cork pads on the other keys too, making the sound a little brighter. Bass clarinets often have cork pads on the register key and other, smaller keys.

Leather
The other pads of most larger clarinets are made of very thin goat (kid) leather. German clarinets often have leather pads as well, to make for a slightly darker timbre than 'fish-skin' pads do. These leather pads, too, are increasingly being replaced by plastic.

Resonators
Some clarinets have metal *resonators* in the pads of the last keys of the lower joint; these slightly enhance brightness and projection.

THE A CLARINET
Clarinetists in a symphony orchestra will almost always have two clarinets: a B-flat clarinet and a slightly longer A clarinet, sounding a half-tone (half-step) lower. An A clarinet also has a slightly different timbre, and in certain keys is a lot easier to play. For instance, a piece in A major concert pitch has five sharps for a B-flat clarinet, and none at all for an A clarinet. If you're playing the latter instrument, you simply play this piece in C major.

Different?
The A clarinet is said to sound a little sweeter, darker, milder, mellower, or richer than a B-flat clarinet. Some clarinetists think the difference is quite marked, others say you only really hear it well at the bottom end of the highest register. Similarly, many composers insist that an A clarinet or a B-flat clarinet be used for specific compositions, while others tend to leave it to the clarinetist.

GERMAN CLARINETS
In Germany and Austria, most clarinetists play 'German clarinets'. These have a slightly different sound, and also a different mechanism. This mechanism comes in many different variations. Albert, Oehler, and reform-Boehm

are the three best known systems. Getting to know a little about these instruments may help gain insight into the French clarinet as well.

Sound

German clarinets sound different from French ones. How different? You often read that German clarinets sound darker, more robust, thicker, fuller, or sweeter, with the French (Boehm) sound being described as brighter, lighter, more open, and more delicate – and of course some clarinetists will say just the opposite.

Different bore

The difference in sound between German and French (Boehm) clarinets lies largely in the bore. One main difference is that German clarinets begin to flare out beyond only the E/B key, rather than halfway down the lower joint. In other words, the cylindrical section of the bore is much longer than on a French instrument. The mouthpiece and reed are different too, as you can read in the chapters that follow.

Wider or narrower?

You often hear that the bore of German clarinets is wider than that of French clarinets – or the opposite, that it is narrower. The truth is that bores vary from brand to brand. While one German clarinet maker uses a narrow bore of around 0.575" (14.6 mm), which is slightly narrower than most French ones, another chooses a wide bore of 0.590" (15 mm), which is as wide as the widest French bore. So it's not the exact

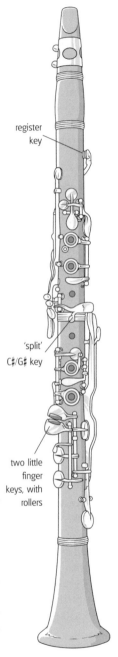

register key

'split' C♯/G♯ key

two little finger keys, with rollers

A German clarinet with the Albert system.

width of the bore at a certain point that makes the difference, but the entire bore, from the top to the bottom of the instrument.

Little fingers' keys
The easiest way to tell you're looking at a German clarinet is by the right little finger keys. There are only two of them, with a roller to help you move from key to key. The left little finger keys are different from the ones on a French clarinet too.

Split and bowed
If you look carefully you'll notice other differences too: For instance, the C-sharp/G-sharp key has a 'split' design, which allows you to operate it with your right little finger as well. The lever of the register key has a large bow in it, as the hole it covers is near the front of the tube, instead of at the back.

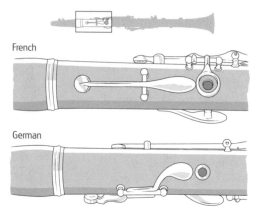

French

German

On German clarinets, the register key lever has been moved nearer the front of the tube.

Albert system
German clarinets come with various different mechanisms. In Germany and Austria, students usually start out on an instrument with the *Albert system*, which has nineteen or twenty keys, and between four, five, or six ring keys.

Oehler system
Most advanced and professional German clarinetists play instruments with the *Oehler system*. You can recognize an

Oehler clarinet by the one plateau key by the right middle finger, and by the two F-resonance keys on the lower joint. Those two extra keys make the F and the low B-flat brighter, and better in tune.

Full-Oehler
Oehler clarinets come in all kinds of variations. The simplest version has twenty-one keys, and so-called *full-Oehlers* may have as many as twenty-seven.

Why French?
The French system is favored in most countries around the world because it is easier to play than the German one. For example, you need fewer fork fingerings , and there are more notes you can play in different ways.

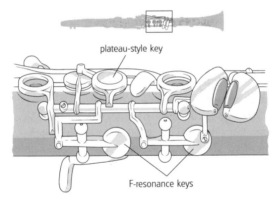

plateau-style key

F-resonance keys

The Oehler system is easy to recognize by the plateau-style key by the right middle finger and the two F-resonance keys on the side.

German with French
The *reform-Boehm* or *German Boehm* clarinet allows you to play with a French mechanism but still sound German. This type of clarinet has a German bore, and hence a German sound, but a French (Boehm) mechanism. The keywork can be slightly different on a few points; for instance, it may have a double F/C key, or rollers between the right little finger keys.

Even more systems
There are many other, lesser known systems as well, such as the Schmidt-Kolbe system, with lots of additional keys,

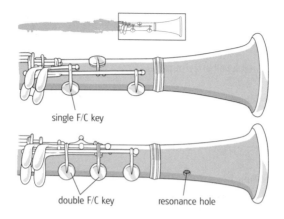

single F/C key

double F/C key   resonance hole

A regular Boehm clarinet with a single F/C key, and a German Boehm with a double F/C key and a resonance hole.

or the old Müller system. Clarinets with these systems are hardly found outside central Europe. In Austria, clarinet players use *Austrian clarinets*, with a wide bore and a mechanism that varies slightly from the Oehler system.

German system

In Germany, the Albert system is known as the *German system*, the other two being referred to with their specific names (*i.e.*, Oehler and reform-Boehm). The name Albert is only really used outside Germany.

IN TUNE

In order to really play a clarinet in tune, you need to correct certain notes even on the best instrument. The better the clarinet, the more inherently in tune it will be, and the less correcting you need to do. In other words, the better a clarinet's intonation, the easier it will be to play in tune.

Out of tune

To judge a clarinet's intonation you need to be able to play pretty well. If not, you'll never know whether it's the clarinet or you that is out of tune.

Too small, too big

A clarinet could only be made completely in tune if it had three or more register keys, and that would make the mechanism much too complicated. So there's only one, and that one register key can never be in the right position for all tone combinations (E/B, F/C, and so on).

Tuning ratios
The exact placement of the tonehole of the register key influences the *tuning ratios* of the instrument: the pitch differences between E/B, F/C, and so on.

Always different
It's not just the register key that determines the intonation of a clarinet. Other factors include the positions and shapes of the toneholes, the bore, the barrel, and the mouthpiece. Every manufacturer chooses its own solutions to make the intonation of its clarinets as good as possible. So which notes you have to correct and by how much can vary from one brand to another, and even from one model to another.

All the same
This is one reason why many groups and orchestras prefer all their clarinetists to play the same type of clarinet – that way, the entire clarinet section is more likely to sound as a whole.

All different
Every clarinet is different. Take that into account when you are play-testing clarinets. If you are used to a clarinet on which a certain note always tends to sound flat (too low), that note may suddenly seem sharp (too high) on a 'better' clarinet because you are compensating too much for it. That can make a good clarinet sound as if it has bad intonation.

Only a few
There are only a few notes that are either sharp (*e.g.*, B4 and C5) or flat (*e.g.*, E3, F3, F2) on just about every clarinet. There are also some notes that are sharp on most clarinets, but flat on others. This is particularly true of the notes you play with most of the keys open, *i.e.*, the highest four notes of the chalumeau register (G4 and up). These are called the *short-pipe* or *short-tube notes*, because you only use a 'short' section of the clarinet to play them.

Too short, too low...

Sometimes, certain notes may be sharp or flat by such an amount that you'll never get them in tune. Some probable causes? Having the wrong mouthpiece on the instrument, or a barrel that's too long or too short, or certain keys open too far, or not far enough... A key that doesn't open far enough can make certain notes sound flat and stuffy. If the *key opening* or *venting* is too big, some notes will be sharp.

LISTENING AND PLAY-TESTING

A good clarinet needs to have a beautiful tone – and what counts as beautiful depends mainly on your taste and the type of music you play. A clarinet should also have an even timbre and tuning, whether you play soft or loud, high or low, and long-tube or short-tube notes.

Another player

In order to choose a clarinet by its sound, you need to be able to play at least reasonably well. If you can't play yet or haven't been playing very long, take a good clarinetist with you to try out the following listening and play-testing tips, or go to a store that employs one.

Somebody else

If you get somebody else to play a bunch of clarinets for you, they'll never sound the same as if you were to play them yourself – but you will be able to hear the differences between the instruments. A tip: Even if you do play yourself, ask somebody else to play for you just to hear how the various clarinets sound from a distance. You'll find that you hear things you didn't hear before. If there's no other clarinetist available, you can point the instruments at a wall so that their sound is reflected back to you.

Same barrel, same mouthpiece

Only if you play every clarinet with the same mouthpiece and barrel will you hear the differences between clarinets – rather than the differences between mouthpieces and barrels. Preferably use your own mouthpiece and barrel to start with, but be aware that some clarinets will perform better with a different combination.

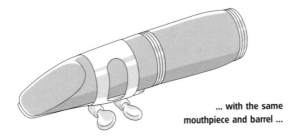

... with the same
mouthpiece and barrel ...

Briefly at first

If you have a whole selection of clarinets in front of you, choosing is often easiest if you only play each instrument briefly. Play something simple, otherwise you'll be concentrating more on playing than on listening. Scales, for instance, nice and slowly. A tip: It may be that you prefer the sound of one clarinet to all the others straight away. That'll often be the clarinet you end up buying.

Two by two

Once you've found a number of clarinets that you really like, compare them two by two or three by three. Choose the best one and replace the one you like least with another clarinet. Again choose the best one, and so on.

A little longer

In order to choose the very best clarinet from the two or three that remain, you may want to play each instrument a little longer so that you get to know it better. A tip: Even after just fifteen minutes of playing it gets harder to hear the differences between clarinets. Take a break, or come back a day or two later.

With your ears alone

Another tip: Try listening to the same clarinets without looking to see which one you're playing. This lets you choose with your ears alone, without being influenced by the price, the brand name or anything else. If the clarinet that sounds best and plays best turns out to be the cheapest one, that's a bonus. Unless you particularly wanted a more expensive one, of course...

Sheet music

If you don't know any music by heart, take a few pieces

with you when you go to choose a clarinet. The better you know a piece, the less you will be thinking about the notes, and the better you can listen.

No idea
If you have no idea where to start when you walk into a store, ask for two clarinets with very different sounds. One with a notably dark tone and another that sounds particularly bright, for example. Decide what you like best and go on from there. Or try a very cheap clarinet alongside the most expensive one in the store, simply to hear how much difference it makes.

Your own clarinet
Take your own clarinet with you to the store, if you have one. That makes it easier to hear just how different instruments sound. On the other hand: You may be so used to your own instrument that it may seem to sound better or more in tune than other clarinets – even much more expensive and better ones.

WHAT TO LISTEN FOR
Comparing sounds is something you have to learn how to do; the more often you do it, the more you hear. It also helps if you know what kind of things you can listen out for – and you can read about that below.

What you like
When two people listen to the same clarinet, they often use very different words to describe what they hear. What one considers shrill and thin (and so not attractive), another may consider bright or brilliant (and so not unattractive). And what one describes as dark and velvety, another may think dull or stuffy. It all depends on what you like, and on the words you use to describe it.

Character
What sounds good and what doesn't also depends on the kind of music you play. If you play classical music, you're probably looking for a darker, warmer sound than if you play jazz or folk music. Some clarinets allow you to play different styles easier than others, being less versatile.

Easy

Some clarinets blow more easily than others. That's mainly to do with the bore. A clarinet with little blowing resistance plays easily and usually has a big, open tone. Classical players generally prefer an instrument with more resistance and a darker sound. If a clarinet has too much resistance, the sound will become dull, stuffy or lifeless.

Resistance

When you play long-tube notes you'll always feel more resistance or pressure than when you play short-tube ones. That difference is bigger with some clarinets than others. The smaller the difference, the easier it is to make the instrument sound even, whether you're playing high, low, short-tube, or long-tube notes. Right-hand notes should not have much more resistance than left-hand notes.

High and low

The high notes sound different from the low ones on all clarinets, but the better the instrument, the smaller the difference will be. The low notes should sound firm, deep, and clear, even when you're playing softly. The high notes must not sound shrill, edgy, or metallic, even when you're playing loudly.

Loud and soft

To test a clarinet, go from high to low playing loudly, and then do the same playing softly. Notice whether the instrument responds equally easily, whether you make each note sound separately (staccato) or join all the notes together (legato).

Rising and falling

When you go from loud to soft, and the other way around, check that the pitch doesn't change too much. On clarinets, the pitch has a tendency to fall as you get louder, and to rise when you get softer. Funny: With most other instruments it's the other way around.

Problem notes   Tipcode CLR-007

When you are comparing the sounds of different clarinets, pay special attention to the highest notes of the chalumeau register (see page 9). Those are the clarinet's 'problem notes'

– the notes which for clarinet makers are hardest to get sounding good. The B-flat is particularly tricky. If that note sounds really good, you're likely to have a great clarinet in your hands. This group of tricky short-tube notes is known as the *throat register* or the *break register*.

SECONDHAND

When you go to buy a secondhand clarinet, there are a few extra things you should remember. To begin with, always put the clarinet together yourself, so you can check that the fit between the sections isn't too tight or too loose. They should fit together so snugly that the clarinet feels as though it was made from a single piece of wood.

Leaky

Check that all notes respond well. If not, there's a fair chance that air is leaking somewhere. That could be down to a torn pad, a poorly adjusted ring or key, or a leak between two joints. Air can also escape from around the register tube. A tip: Take off the upper joint, close all the toneholes, and block one end with your hand. Then put your lips around the other end, and suck. If you inhale any air, there is a leak somewhere. Do the same with the lower joint – and you can blow instead if you want to. When you blow hard, the C-sharp and E-flat keys on the lower joint may open of their own accord. If so, their springs should be adjusted to provide a little more resistance.

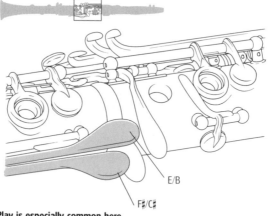

E/B

F♯/C♯

Play is especially common here.

Wobble

Tipcode CLR-008

Check carefully whether keys and levers can only move up and down, not sideways or back and forth. Older instruments often suffer from wobble on the F-sharp/C-sharp and the E/B by the left little finger. Wobble makes playing uncomfortable, and it may cause leaks and noise. What's more, it always gets worse.

Noise

Noise and buzzing sounds may also be due to poor adjustment, a missing cork, torn pads, loose or missing springs, or a loose metal bell ring, tenon ring, or body ring. If a ring is loose, it may be that the clarinet has been stored in a room with very low air humidity, which increases the chances that the wood will crack – now or later.

Cracks

Wooden clarinets always need to be checked for cracks. The most likely places to find cracks are the tenons, and the toneholes by the A, A-flat, and trill keys. Small cracks can often be effectively repaired.

The bore

Look down through the bore, and do the same with the barrel and the mouthpiece. If the previous owner took good care of the instrument, everything will look smooth on the inside and it will smell only of clarinet.

Mouthpiece

Also inspect the outside of the mouthpiece. If there are teeth marks in it, your own teeth will naturally be forced into the same position. Check the edges too: Even minor damage can make a mouthpiece unusable. In the following chapter you will read why even a good mouthpiece with slight damage may be no use to you.

Appraisal

It's always a good idea to have a used clarinet appraised by an expert. Then you'll know what it's worth, and what it may cost you to have it adjusted or repaired. To give you an idea: A crack can often be repaired for around fifty dollars, and for some four to five hundred dollars or more you may get an old, worn-out clarinet made as good as new.

6. MOUTHPIECES, LIGATURES, AND BARRELS

How a clarinet plays depends more than anything else on who is playing it. Almost as important to the sound are the reed, which you can read all about in Chapter 7, the mouthpiece and the barrel – and even the ligature plays a role.

Some mouthpieces are easier to play than others. If you are just starting out, it's nice to have one that plays easily–though a mouthpiece like that usually won't get you the dark tone that many clarinetists are after. If you've been playing a little longer, the best mouthpiece is one that allows you to play loudly and softly, high and low, and staccato and legato with equal ease and a balanced, stable timbre and pitch.

The clarinet

You can't simply put any mouthpiece on any clarinet. A poorly chosen mouthpiece will 'fit,' but it can make the instrument sound out of tune, edgy, dull, or unbalanced.

You

A mouthpiece also has to suit you. That includes your embouchure, your technique, and the sound you are looking for. One person may play beautifully with a mouthpiece that another has trouble getting a decent note out of.

Almost everybody

Then there are mouthpieces that almost everybody feels comfortable with. Such mouthpieces are often used in orchestras or groups in which all the clarinetists play the same brand of instrument.

A good replacement

These 'user-friendly' mouthpieces also make a good first replacement for the cheap mouthpieces that come with cheap clarinets. Real cheap mouthpieces will make most instruments sound edgy and harsh, and they're often quite hard to play – which can make half an hour's practice seem like a very long time...

Keep looking

Also, one of these user-friendly mouthpieces will give you a good starting point if you later decide to try out some more different ones. And there's enough to choose from, right up to hand-made mouthpieces that cost more than two hundred dollars. The cheapest models cost about twenty to thirty dollars, and mouthpieces used by professionals start around seventy-five to a hundred.

In brief

When you go out to buy a mouthpiece, you're bound to come across the following terms:

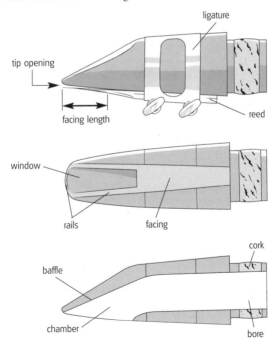

A mouthpiece shown from the side, from below and in cross-section.

- The *tip opening* is the space between the tip of the reed and the tip of the mouthpiece.
- The *facing length* is the distance from the tip opening to where the reed first touches the mouthpiece. It's not just the length of the facing (or *lay*) that matters, but also its curvature.
- The opening that is closed off by the reed is called the *window* or *wind cut*. Behind the window is the *chamber*.
- The other end, where the mouthpiece connects with the barrel, is the *bore*.

Dimensions or words?

Mouthpiece brochures usually tell you the exact sizes of the tip opening and facing length of each mouthpiece. On their own, these figures don't tell you too much: A mouthpiece has many more dimensions that affect its performance. So it's usually more useful to read what a brochure says about the sound you can expect from a certain mouthpiece, and about the style of music for which it has been designed. A very subdued sound, for instance, for chamber music. Or a sound that blends well, for symphonic work. Lots of volume and projection, for orchestras that play outdoors, or great flexibility, for jazz.

Different brand, different sound

Each mouthpiece brand has its own 'character'. The mouthpieces of Brand A may sound very direct, bright or edgy, Brand B may be a little warmer, while those of Brand C offer more resistance and a darker timbre. Which brands fit those descriptions usually depends on who you ask…

Easy

Some clarinetists spend their whole lives looking for the ideal mouthpiece. Others are much less demanding, or they have an 'easy embouchure' – it doesn't matter much which mouthpiece they use, and reeds pretty much always work fine for them as well.

One or more

Similarly, there are clarinetists who use one and the same mouthpiece for all kinds of different musical styles, and others who use two, three or more different mouthpieces, each with its own character.

Knitted cord

German clarinets have very different mouthpieces to French ones, with smaller tip openings and longer facings. The reed is usually not attached with a ligature but bound on with a knitted cord. Some 'French' players use that method too.

German on French

If you fit a German mouthpiece on a French clarinet, you'll immediately hear how much influence the mouthpiece has on the sound: It makes a French clarinet sound very 'German.' While some experts tend to disapprove of doing so, other clarinetists always use this particular combination – that may take a slight modification of the mouthpiece or the barrel.

Mouthpiece tips

If you are going out to choose a new mouthpiece, the following tips may be of use:

- Make sure you know roughly **what you are looking for**. A good salesperson will then be able to recommend a handful of mouthpieces, so that you won't have to try dozens.
- Take **your own clarinet and mouthpiece** with you for comparison.
- If you always use a **mouthpiece cushion** (see page 69), don't test other mouthpieces without one. A mouthpiece cushion also prevents you leaving tooth marks in new mouthpieces.
- Don't compare twenty different mouthpieces at once. Instead, **choose three**, listen, and replace the one you like least with another. And so on.
- Take **breaks**: After a quarter of an hour of testing you won't be able to hear what you're doing nearly as well.
- Choosing the perfect mouthpiece quickly will always be difficult: You only really get to know a new mouthpiece **after a few weeks' playing**.
- Also, a mouthpiece won't perform to its full potential until you have found the right reed to go with it. A good salesperson can advise you on **good reed/mouthpiece combinations**.
- When you are testing mouthpieces, be sure to always use a **good, new reed**.

- When it comes to mouthpieces, **thousandths of an inch** can make a difference. That's why no two mouthpieces are exactly the same. Even if you know exactly which mouthpiece you want, it's still worth trying out a few of the same type: There's a good chance you'll like one better than another.

THE DIFFERENCES

How a mouthpiece plays and sounds depends on the tip opening, the length and curvature of the facing, the material, and much else besides.

Names and numbers

Almost all manufacturers use combinations of letters and numbers to identify their different mouthpieces. Sadly, those 'codes' usually tell you nothing. For instance, with one brand a higher number means a larger tip opening, with another it means a smaller one.

Similar mouthpiece, different code

As an example, the Vandoren B45, the Leblanc L4, and the Selmer 120 are three comparable mouthpieces – but you wouldn't think so if you only looked at their codes. There are only a few brands that print the dimensions of the tip, the facing and the chamber on their mouthpieces.

Tables

To make your quest a bit easier, there are tables listing the characteristics of mouthpieces by different brands side by side. You may find these tables on the Internet and in music stores.

The whole thing

Everything to do with mouthpieces is interrelated. For instance, two mouthpieces with the same tip opening and the same facing length may nevertheless sound and play very differently. Or one of them may work brilliantly on one clarinet and terribly on another. In the end, it's a matter of trying them out until you find the perfect combination, in which clarinet, mouthpiece, reed, barrel, and ligature together sound and play exactly the way you want them to.

TIP OPENING

When it comes to tip openings, thousandths of an inch count. Most French mouthpieces have openings of between 0.039" and 0.047" (1–1.2 mm).

Beginners and all-rounders

Many beginners choose a mouthpiece with a tip opening of around 0.045"; not too big (to avoid pitch fluctuations), and not too small (because you'd need too much air). A versatile mouthpiece that suits clarinetists in all kinds of different styles is likely to have a similar, medium-sized tip opening.

Small

A smaller tip opening usually means a darker sound and more resistance. A small opening also requires a harder reed – if the reed were too soft it would vibrate over too great a distance. Since a harder reed doesn't move up and down as far, pitch and sound are not as easy to adjust. If the tip opening is too small, the result may be a dull, stuffy tone, a sharp pitch, and an exhausted player.

Large

A large tip opening makes playing easier, it opens up the sound, and you get more volume and a more vivid tone. There's a lot of scope for correcting tone and pitch, allowing you to slide from note to note, for instance. The fact that you *can* correct more also means you always *have to* correct more. With a large tip opening you need a flexible reed, which can vibrate far enough. The biggest tip opening is just under 0.060" (1.5 mm) – but such mouthpieces are rare.

Converting

American brands usually give tip openings in thousandths of an inch. If you want to convert a 'European' tip opening, given in hundredths of a millimeter, to inches, divide by 25.4. An example: A tip opening 127 is actually 1.27 mm, and 1.27 ÷ 25.4 = 0.050". The other way around: an American size 50 would be 50 x 0.0254 = 1.27 mm.

Other clarinets

Mouthpieces for larger and smaller clarinets naturally have

larger and smaller tip openings, respectively. To give you an idea: The tip opening of a bass clarinet mouthpiece is usually somewhere between 0.060" and 0.080" (1.5–2 mm).

THE FACING

On its own, the facing length doesn't tell you very much. It's the combination of the facing length and the tip opening that's really important. An example: A small tip opening with a long facing gives a good response, with a dark, rich tone. But if you combine that same facing length with a large tip opening, you will get a brighter tone and more volume.

Curvature and facing

At least as important is curvature of the facing, though brochures tell you next to nothing about that. The main reason is that it is not easy to describe how 'curved' a facing is.

All-purpose facing

The term *facing* is also used to indicate the length and the curvature of the lay, as well as the tip opening, which are closely related of course. A mouthpiece with an *all-purpose facing* has a medium-sized tip opening and a medium-length facing that is neither too curved nor too flat.

Long or short

On French mouthpieces, the facing length typically varies between about 0.710" and 0.865" (18–22 mm). A longer facing allows for a broader, bigger sound; a shorter facing is more likely to produce a more focused, centered sound.

Words or letters

The facing length is often indicated using words or letters rather than figures. A tip: What one brand calls short, another brand may call medium.

The rails

The edges or *rails* of the mouthpiece are also part of the facing. If the *side rails* are not exactly the same shape and thickness, the mouthpiece will be out of balance. As a result, you may get squeaks, or your instrument may have a poor response or a shrill sound.

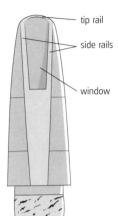

tip rail

side rails

window

Sound

The thickness of the side rails and the *tip rail* also affect the tone. Thicker rails make the sound thicker and darker, while narrower edges give a brighter sound. If the rails are too thick, the sound becomes dull; if they are too narrow, it'll be harsh or edgy.

Wear

Most mouthpieces are made of hard rubber. This material is less hard than it appears, and hard rubber mouthpieces actually wear out in time. One cause is cleaning, another is that the reed constantly beats the mouthpiece when you play: A clarinet has what is officially known as a *beating reed*. If you're finding it very hard to find a reed that works with your instrument, or if your tone is growing shrill and harsh, try a new mouthpiece; you may find out your old one has worn out.

CHAMBER, BAFFLE, BORE, AND TABLE

A mouthpiece with a large chamber has a dark, warm, full sound that is especially well suited to classical music. For a bright, vivid sound with a good projection, you're usually better off with a mouthpiece that has a smaller chamber.

Baffle

Some mouthpieces have a *baffle* (see illustration on page 61). This lowering of the chamber's 'ceiling' (the *palate*) compresses the air, making the sound brighter and increasing the projection. Conversely, a concave palate would make the sound darker.

Bore

There are special mouthpieces for instruments with large or narrow bores, but you don't usually need to pay special attention to the bore of the mouthpiece itself. If you are interested, though, the effect of the mouthpiece bore is comparable to that of the bore of the instrument: A narrow bore gives a tighter, more focused, and darker sound, and a wide bore a 'wider,' more open sound.

Table

The table, upon which the reed rests, is usually flat. On some mouthpieces, it is a tiny bit concave when looked at lengthwise. This slight depression is supposed to allow the reed to vibrate more freely, which in turn enables you to influence the sound a little more, whether by the tension of your lips or by your choice of ligature (see page 73).

Beaks and bites

Mouthpieces differ in many other ways – the *beak angle* may vary, for instance. That means that the part you set your teeth on is either steeper or less steep than normal, making the mouthpiece feel either fatter or thinner. There are also mouthpieces that have been specially adapted for clarinetists with overbite or underbite.

MATERIALS

Most clarinetists use hard rubber (ebonite) mouthpieces. Alternatively, you can get mouthpieces made of plastic, crystal, metal, wood or other materials.

Ebonite

Ebonite mouthpieces tend to offer a fairly warm, dark sound, but there are some that can make your sound edgy and bright. The difference is due partly to the hardness of the ebonite, and partly to the shape of the mouthpiece.

Plastic

Plastic is mainly, but not exclusively, used for cheap mouthpieces. The sound is often quite hard and bright.

Crystal, glass, and metal

Most crystal mouthpieces are designed to generate a dark, warm sound, but some actually sound quite bright. Crystal is very fragile, of course. Glass and metal mouthpieces are very rare.

Wood

Most wooden mouthpieces make clarinets sound extra dark and round. Because no two pieces of wood are the same, there can be big variations between two 'identical' mouthpieces. Wooden mouthpieces also react quickly to changes in temperature and air humidity.

Mouthpiece cushions

Most clarinetists use mouthpiece cushions on their mouthpieces. A cushion protects the mouthpiece from your teeth, and your teeth from the vibration of the mouthpiece. The soft synthetic layer also gives you a bit of extra grip on the mouthpiece.

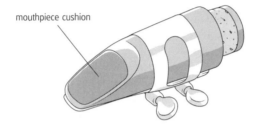

mouthpiece cushion

The sound

Even a mouthpiece cushion can affect the sound – especially the sound as you hear it yourself, because less of the sound is transmitted directly through your teeth. Also, the sound may be altered very slightly because a mouthpiece cushion makes you open your mouth a fraction further. Mouthpiece cushions come in different thicknesses and hardnesses, and some brands adhere better than others. Try a few different ones and then decide which one you like best – they're not expensive. You can buy them separately or in sets.

GERMAN MOUTHPIECES

German mouthpieces have a much smaller tip opening (approximately 0.025–0.040" or 0.65–1 mm) than French ones, and a longer facing length (from around 0.730"–0.985" or 18.5–25 mm, or more).

Window and walls

German mouthpieces have a narrower window than French mouthpieces. If you look through a German mouthpiece, you'll see that the side-walls get slightly further apart towards the bottom of the chamber. These *angled side-walls* are said to make the sound, which is focused or centered by the narrow window, a bit 'broader.' Straight side-walls, on the other hand, are said to enhance the projection and make the sound less warm.

Cord
Tipcode CLR-009

The ligature is different too. German clarinetists still often bind their reeds to the mouthpiece with a cord. In order to provide the cord some extra hold, the mouthpiece has grooves around it.

MOUTHPIECE BRANDS

There are scores of mouthpiece brands. Vandoren, which also makes reeds, is the biggest. Most clarinet brands have their own mouthpieces, which they don't always make themselves. Ernst Schreiber is just one example of a manufacturer that makes mouthpieces for lots of other companies besides its own ESM mouthpieces. Many of the other manufacturers are small companies, that often focus on more expensive mouthpieces, such as Charles Bay, Blayman, Gigliotti, Lakey, Mitchell Lurie, Morgan, Pomarico, Pyne, Runyib, Rovner, and Woodwind. Companies like Bilger, Brilhart, Combs, Fobes, Hite, and Jewel also have more affordable mouthpieces. Mouthpieces with a Viotto facing are made in Germany. Many small makers use mouthpiece blanks by the firm Zinner as a basis for their own products.

BARRELS

The barrel or *socket* is primarily used to tune the clarinet, but it also has a significant influence on the sound, ease of playing, and intonation.

Two barrels

Many clarinets in the higher price ranges come with two barrels, one of them 0.40" or 0.80" (1 or 2 mm) longer than the other. The longer barrel makes the instrument sound just a little lower; the shorter one makes it sound a bit higher.

Shorter higher, longer lower

You might use that shorter barrel if you were playing with an orchestra that tunes slightly higher, or if it's very cold and your instrument is sounding a bit too low, or if you are a 'flat' clarinetist: Some clarinetists play slightly flatter than others, even with exactly the same instrument, mouthpiece, and reed. If you buy a new mouthpiece that sounds just a little higher or lower than the old one, a longer or shorter barrel can compensate for the difference.

Preferably longer

Some clarinetists prefer the longest barrel they can use while still playing in tune, because they say even those few tenths of an inch make their sound just a little deeper and warmer.

Too long, too short

The length of the barrel has a greater effect on the pitch of the notes from the upper part of the clarinet (the short-tube notes) than on the other notes. So if you choose a barrel that is too long, those short-tube notes will become much too low compared to the other notes. If your barrel is too short, on the other hand, the short-tube notes will be too high compared to the others. Barrels can be too long or too short even if they differ from the original barrel by some 0.060" (1.5 mm).

Adjustable

Adjustable barrels are also available. They usually go from approximately 2.35" to 3.25" (60–80 mm) in length. But of course, you can only use about 0.120" (3 mm) of that range before the barrel becomes either too long or too short to still play in tune.

Thick and thin

Separate barrels not only come in different lengths, but also in different thicknesses and materials,

An adjustable barrel
(Click Tuning Barrel).

and with different bores. A barrel with a thicker wall gives a 'thicker,' darker, heavier, fuller sound. A clarinet with a thin wall barrel responds more easily, and has a brighter, lighter sound.

Material

Cheaper wooden clarinets often have a plastic bell and barrel. If you replace the barrel with a wooden one, the sound can audibly improve. Besides barrels made of grenadilla, you can get all kinds of unusual designs in bronze or special wood varieties, or wooden barrels with an ebonite lining for a somewhat brighter sound.

Bore

The bore is also important. Barrels with cylindrical bores sound wider and more open than barrels whose bores narrow steadily toward the bottom: A *reverse taper* produces a warmer, more focused sound. There are many other variations, each of which has its own effect on the sound, the intonation (especially that of the short-tube notes), and the response of the instrument. Some barrels even have interchangeable bores.

Hard to predict

Exactly how a barrel will influence the tone of your instrument is hard to predict: It depends to a large extent on how you play, your mouthpiece, the reed, and the instrument itself.

Brands

Each clarinet brand has its own barrels. In addition, there are a few specialized barrel brands, of which Chadash and Moennig are the best known.

NECKS

Larger clarinets, such as the alto and the bass, have a metal neck instead of a barrel. This neck or *bocal* is used to tune the instrument. Some necks consist of two sections that you fix together with a screw. Other types use cork tenons like an ordinary clarinet. Some brands supply one shorter and one longer neck to go with each instrument, just as you sometimes get two barrels with a soprano clarinet.

From the front

When you play a bass clarinet, the mouthpiece enters your mouth at a different angle to that of an ordinary clarinet: more from the front, instead of from below. That can make things difficult for clarinetists who play both instruments and often need to swap between them. A solution is to buy a special bass clarinet neck that is bent in such a way that the mouthpiece enters your mouth a little closer to the vertical.

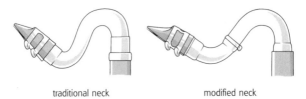

traditional neck   modified neck

With the special neck (right), the mouthpiece enters your mouth at a different angle.

LIGATURES

Even the ligature contributes to your sound. The differences lie mainly in how the reed is held in place and in the material of the ligature.

One or two

Many ligatures have two screws. Although that takes a little more work, it does ensure a good distribution of pressure across the reed. Other ligatures have been designed to do the same job with a single screw.

Inverted

An *inverted ligature* has screws not at the bottom of the mouthpiece but on top. This supposedly allows the reed to move more freely, and so respond more easily.

Material

Besides conventional metal ligatures, there are models in leather, soft plastic, textile, or metal mesh. The softer and thicker the material, the darker and more velvety the sound often becomes. The same happens if you secure the reed with a cord, as many German clarinetists do. A 'soft' ligature of this kind is also said to make the sound more flexible and darker.

A metal ligature and a soft one.

Spots or strips

A very different effect is produced if the reed is held in place only by a few metal points or thin, metal strips. The less material touches the reed, the more freely it can vibrate; that usually makes the sound brighter and more open, and makes the instrument respond more easily. Other ligatures have adjustable clamp systems, so that you can adapt the sound to the music, the venue, or the ensemble.

Tips and tricks

You can also adjust simple ligatures to some extent. If you have a reed that is actually too light, tighten the upper screw a bit less. That allows a longer section of the reed to vibrate, which has an effect similar to that of a slightly heavier reed. There are more tips and tricks in Chapter 8, *Before and After*.

Bite

Another point to watch out for: Some types of ligature allow you to vary the exact position of the reed very easily, even without (re)moving the ligature itself. Others don't. Another difference is that some ligatures 'bite' into the reed. This means that you'll only be able to fix the reed in that same position from then on.

Prices

The cheapest standard ligatures are available for five to ten dollars. Expect to pay ten to twenty if you want something better, and twice to four times that amount if you want something special. Almost all clarinet and mouthpiece brands have their own ligatures, and there are also specialist brands such as B&G, Oleg, Tru-Blo, and Winslow. A tip: A different ligature usually requires a different *mouthpiece cap*.

7. REEDS

What strings are to guitarists and violinists, reeds are to a clarinetist. They are important for the way you sound and the way you play, you need to replace them frequently, and there are all kinds of tricks to make them last as long as possible.

The main difference between one reed and the other is how soft or hard they are. The softest reeds are used mainly by beginners, and on mouthpieces with large tip openings. To use a hard reed, which you'll find especially on mouthpieces with small tip openings, you need to be able to play well. You can tell how hard or soft a reed is by its number.

Numbers
Most manufacturers use the numbers 1 to 5, often in half steps. The higher the number, the harder or more resistant the reed.

Harder
A harder reed gives a heavier, darker, thicker or fuller sound. It's not as easy to correct the pitch when playing with a hard reed – but that also means that playing louder or softer will not result in pitch variations that easily. A hard reeds makes it harder to play low pitches softly.

Softer
With a softer reed playing softly is easier. A soft read speaks more easily, and gives a bright, lighter sound, but there is a greater chance that the pitch will go up and down as you play, so it's harder to play in tune.

Equally thick

A higher number means that the reed is harder, being cut from a harder, less flexible piece of cane. It will be exactly the same thickness as a reed that has a lower number, assuming it's the same type of reed.

Two?

Another tip: What one brand calls a number 2 may be equivalent to a 1½ or a 2½ reed from another brand, and the same variation can be found within different series of one brand. As with mouthpieces, there are tables that list various brands and series side by side. Some brands use names (*i.e.* soft, medium, hard, etc.) instead of numbers.

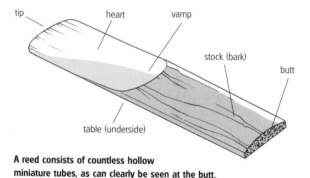

A reed consists of countless hollow miniature tubes, as can clearly be seen at the butt.

In a box

Almost every box of reeds contains great reeds and good reeds, average and poor ones. If the boxes you buy seem to contain fewer and fewer good reeds, try a different brand or a different type – and be sure that the problem doesn't lie somewhere else. If your mouthpiece is crooked or damaged, for instance, any reed will seem poor.

Not equally hard

Of course, ten 'identical' reeds from one and the same box won't all be equally hard either. A box of reeds number 2½ will contain reeds that are just a little harder than a 'hard' 2, as well as some that come close to a 'soft' 3.

Thicker, steeper

How a reed plays and sounds also depends on its shape. The thickness of the heart may vary, the slope towards the edges may be a little steeper or a little more gentle, and so on. For example, some types of reeds are cut a little thicker and make the sound a little tighter, clearer, or more focused.

Filed and unfiled

Reeds with a *file cut* or *double cut* have an extra strip of the bark removed, in a straight line, right behind the vamp. This enhances the flexibility of the reed, making for an easier response, especially in the low register. Also, it helps produce a brighter, more narrowly focused sound. As this technique was developed in France – where classical players have always appreciated a brighter sound than in Germany, say – it's known as *French file cut*. The 'regular' or *unfiled cut* is sometimes referred to as *single cut*.

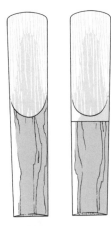

Reeds with and without a (French) file cut.

Fine-tuning

The choice between filed and unfiled reeds can help you fine-tune your sound, regardless of the style in which you're playing. Generally speaking, players with a darker-sounding mouthpiece may prefer filed reeds, while unfiled reeds are often used on mouthpieces that tend to produce a brighter sound.

Which type of reed?

Each brand makes different types of reeds. The only way to find out which reed you like best is to keep trying them out. Trading experiences with other clarinetists helps, but every clarinetist blows differently, and a reed that works brilliantly with one mouthpiece can seem hopeless on another.

Still looking

So if you're still looking, buy reeds of different series, brands, and numbers. Try more than one reed of each type: One poor reed tells you nothing. Most clarinetists who have found 'their' reed buy them in boxes of five or ten. Reeds typically cost between one and a half to two dollars each.

German and Austrian reeds

The reeds you use for a German mouthpiece are cut differently to French reeds: They have a different profile. You often read that you shouldn't use German reeds on a French mouthpiece, or the other way around – but some clarinetists are very positive about such combinations. There are also special mouthpieces and reeds for Austrian (Viennese) players.

LOOKING AND PLAYING

There are all kinds of ways to discover whether a reed is good or not so good, and there are all kinds of tricks to make reeds last as long as possible.

Against the light

If you hold up a reed to the light, you'll see an inverted V. That V must be precisely in the center of the reed, and the reed must get thinner evenly to the left and to the right. 'Crooked' reeds squeak, and they're hard to play.

| Good V-shape: can sound good. | A 'crooked' reed, risk of squeaks. | Uneven grain: better not to buy it. | Knots: reed vibrates unevenly. |

Too young

A good reed is golden yellow to golden brown in color. Reeds with a hint of green are too young: Usually they won't play well, if at all, and won't last long.

Grain and knots

An even grain gives you a better chance of a reed that sounds good than a grain that crosses the reed at different angles. Reeds with spots and knots are unlikely to vibrate evenly.

Wet it first

You won't know how good a reed is until you have been playing it for a while. A dry reed doesn't vibrate properly, so always wet it first. Keep it in your mouth for a while or put it in a glass of lukewarm water for a few minutes. The latter method may extend the life of a reed: Some say water is better for reeds than saliva – but others disagree.

Break them in

Reeds that perform very well straight away often don't last very long. The best reeds are often the ones that seem a little hard to begin with. In other words, they don't initially play well right away. That's why some clarinetists first 'break in' their new reeds, for instance by only using them a few minutes per day for the first week. They may also use that breaking-in period to adjust the reed if necessary – a little bit every day. Other clarinetists never do: If a reed doesn't play well, they simply take a different one.

Double plus, double minus

When you're testing a box of new reeds, give each reed a grade, or give the best reeds two plusses, the worst ones two minuses, and so on. Don't throw away the 'bad' reeds, but leave them for a few months: Sometimes they will improve by themselves, and they never get too old. You can also try adjusting the poorer ones, or experiment a little with the placement of the reed on the mouthpiece (see page 80).

Swapping

Reeds are said to last longer if you don't use the same one for too long at a stretch. Indeed, some clarinetists always have a supply of good reeds on them, so that they can switch reeds every hour or even sooner. Another reason to change reeds is that otherwise your reed will gradually become weaker. By the time the reed 'goes,' it will be so weak that any new reed you try will seem too hard.

Suddenly

If you change reeds regularly, you will also get a better feel for the little differences between reeds. What's more, you'll always have plenty of good reeds on hand – which is useful, because even the best reed can give up suddenly.

Big differences

You can also deliberately use the differences between reeds: For example, you can take a softer-playing reed if the air is very dry, or if the acoustics are dead, and a slightly harder one in humid conditions, or if you are playing a venue with a lot of echo, like a church. Some clarinetists always carry different types of reeds for this purpose.

Tasty

Don't like the taste of cane? Then try some of the flavored reeds available, or buy a bottle of reed flavoring, available in various tastes.

ADJUSTING REEDS

Some clarinetists adjust every reed themselves, others do so only if it is really necessary – or they just don't. Learning to adjust reeds takes a lot of time and, to start with, a lot of reeds too. A few important tips are listed below; some of the books on page 130 discuss this subject at greater length.

Higher, lower, or crooked

Before adjusting a reed, you can first experiment with its exact position on the mouthpiece. A reed that doesn't seem to work well when it is put on perfectly straight may suddenly start sounding good if you mount it a little higher, a little lower, or at a slight angle – in which case adjustment will no longer be necessary. Want to know more? See page 87.

Flat   Tipcode CLR-010

If you have a reed whose *facing* (the part in contact with the mouthpiece) is not perfectly flat or even, you can sand it down. Lay a piece of very fine grade sandpaper (number 320 or finer) on a small plate of glass, to make sure it is level, and draw the reed across it a few times.

You can use a whetstone (*carborundum stone*) instead. Carefully turn the reed, first clockwise, then anticlockwise. Exert as little pressure as possible and don't let the tip touch the stone. Some people scour the reed with a sharp penknife instead, pulling the blade across the reed a few times.

Too soft

A reed that's too soft can leave you with a messy, unsteady tone, or make a tone stop in midair. The solution is to clip off no more than 0.04" to 0.06" (1–1.5 mm) from the tip with a *reed cutter* or *reed trimmer*. First wet the reed. You may need to smooth the corners a little after cutting. Use a file, moving it towards the center of the reed, and only do so if it's necessary. Most reed cutters cost around twenty to fifty dollars.

Too hard

If a reed is too hard, you can make it more flexible by scraping it with a sharp knife or a piece of Dutch rush, for sale in music stores. Start in the area around the figure 1 – carefully, because the reed is already very thin at this point. If necessary, go on to the areas marked 2, then to 3 and 4. Always remove equal amounts left and right, otherwise you will push the reed out of balance.

Shrill or dull

You can try rescuing a shrill-sounding reed by adjusting the areas marked 3 and 4. On dull-sounding reeds you start at 1, then move on to 3 and 4, and possibly try 2 as well.

Squeak

Squeaking reeds are often not equally flexible or equally thick on the left and the right. In the latter case, you can try making the thicker edge a little thinner. Keep checking how much you have removed by blowing with the mouthpiece at an angle in your mouth: First try it left, then right.

Tips

- Work carefully: It's easy to remove **too much material**. For example, taking as little as 0.0004" (¹⁄₁₀₀ mm) from the tip of a reed, makes it a whole 10% thinner!
- Frequently **check your results** as you work. Instead of constantly taking the ligature off and putting it back on again, you can also hold the reed in place with your thumb.

- **Waves at the tip** of the reed will disappear when you play it for a while, or if you briefly put the reed in a glass of water.
- Some reeds will **never be any good**, however much you work on them.
- As a rule, avoid the area marked X, the **heart of the reed**.
- If you want to tackle the job really seriously, you can buy special reed **adjustment devices** with prices up to three hundred dollars.

LIFETIME

A reed consists of countless hollow miniature tubes or fibers with a soft material called pith between them. The *pith* becomes gradually softer from exposure to your saliva, until it gets so soft that the reed stops working altogether. How long that takes depends on the type of saliva you have, how often you play, and on the reed itself. Reeds often last between two and four weeks, but there is this clarinetist who claims to have been using one specific reed for thirteen years, and only when performing Mozart in the summer…

Increasing the lifetime

There are all kinds of ways you can try to increase the useful life of your reeds.

- Rinse your reed **in clean water** after playing. Then dry it, for instance with a cotton cloth or handkerchief, or by passing it between your thumb and index finger, always towards the tip. Some clarinet players just dry the reed, without rinsing it first.
- Always store your reeds in a good **reed case or reed guard** (see pages 91–92).
- Lay each new reed on a flat surface and firmly rub it from the heart to the tip with the back of a teaspoon. This **closes the fibers** in the reed, which enhances its life expectancy.
- Don't play too long **without changing your reed** (see page 79).
- **Break your reeds in**, so that the dried material gradually gets used to being wet again.
- **Hydrogen peroxide** solution (3%, available from your local drugstore) counteracts the effect of your saliva on

the reed. Put your reeds in the solution overnight once in a while, and rinse them well before you use them again.

· **Never** set down a mouthpiece with a reed in it vertically. Lay it on its side, so that it can't fall over. That'll save on broken reeds.

· **Taking a break?** A mouthpiece cap protects your reed and keeps it moist.

Synthetic reeds

Synthetic or plastic reeds are also available – for example, from the brands BARI, Fiberreed, Fibracell, Hahn, Hartmann, Légère, Olivieri, and RKM. Some of their advantages are that they last much longer and they're very consistent: Two 'identical' synthetic reeds really are identical. They're also useful if you play different instruments during a concert: You don't need to wet these reeds first.

Expensive

Synthetic reeds are a good deal more expensive, with prices between five and twenty dollars each. Also, many players feel that they tend to sound shrill, harsh or edgy, but it should be noted that this relatively new type of reeds is still being improved all the time. Besides plastic reeds, there are also cane reeds with a plastic coating and other variations on the theme.

Some brand names

Rico (US) also makes reeds under the LaVoz and Mitchell Lurie names. The companies Brancher, Glotin, Marca, Rigotti, Selmer (which also makes clarinets), and Vandoren (which also makes mouthpieces) are from France, which is where most of the reed cane grows. Some other brand names are Alexander Superial (Japan), Reeds Australia, Peter Ponzol (makes mouthpieces too), RKM, and Zonda.

8. BEFORE AND AFTER

A chapter about all the things you need to do with your clarinet before and after playing: from putting it together and warming it up to tuning it, taking it apart, and drying and storing it, including tips on amplification, stands and lyres. More advanced maintenance is discussed in Chapter 9.

A lot of clarinets get broken by falling out of cases that have been opened the wrong way up. So before opening the case, make sure the lid is at the top. A tip: The lid usually has a logo on it. If not, you can tell which way up the case is by looking at the handle, which is always attached to the bottom half.

Cracks

Wooden clarinets can crack due to rapid changes in temperature and air humidity. If you've been outdoors on a very cold day and you then walk into a warm room, you should allow your clarinet to acclimatize in its case first. You can also warm it up in your hands. Don't start playing until the instrument no longer feels cold to the touch, so that the moisture and warmth of your breath won't shock the material.

Only one way

There's usually only one way to put a clarinet back into its case. Exactly how depends on the design of the case – so have a good look before taking the instrument out. Be especially careful with the upper and lower joints, to avoid bending the keys. One tip: The keys must always face up.

Cork grease

Cork grease makes everything slide more smoothly when you're assembling your clarinet, it keeps the cork of the tenons in good condition, and seals the joints better. You can get it in small pots or in lipstick-style containers, the latter keeping your fingers cleaner. Apple-scented cork grease and other aromas are also available.

Gently   Tipcode CLR-013

There are all kinds of ways to assemble a clarinet. One commonly used method is described below. A tip before

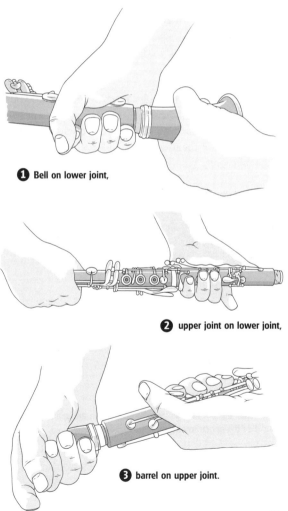

1 Bell on lower joint,

2 upper joint on lower joint,

3 barrel on upper joint.

you start: Don't lift the upper and lower joints out of the case by the keywork. Instead, use a finger to gently lift them up a little by one end, and then get hold of them properly.

Bell on lower joint
First take the lower joint. Hold it as shown in the illustration and attach the bell with a careful twisting movement.

Upper joint on lower joint
Now take hold of the upper joint, resting your fingers on the rings. Press the ring keys down as you attach the upper joint to the lower joint with a careful twisting movement. Hold the lower joint at the bottom end, as shown in the illustration, without squeezing the mechanism. The bell will give you some extra grip.

The bridge   Tipcode CLR-014
To avoid damaging the bridge mechanism, it should be in the 'open' position when you are joining the upper and lower joints together. This is why you should press down the ring keys of the upper joint and *not* press the ones of the lower joint.

Barrel on upper joint
Now slide the barrel onto the upper joint. The easiest way is to rest the bell on the top of your leg, so that you don't have to grip the clarinet too tightly.

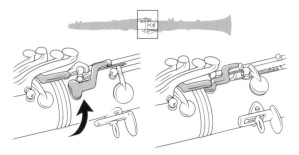

Hold down the D/A ring, so that the bridge is in the open position as you slide the upper and lower joints together.

Mouthpiece
Again, rest the bell against your leg to help you slide the mouthpiece onto the barrel. Next, fit the reed.

In four steps
Tipcode CLR-015

1. Slide the ligature over the mouthpiece until it's almost in its final position.
2. Place the wetted reed (see page 79) under the ligature…
3. … and make sure the edges and the tip are exactly in line with the rails and tip of the mouthpiece.
4. Now slide the ligature into place and tighten it – not too much, otherwise the reed won't vibrate properly.

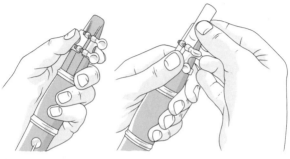

1 First the ligature...   2 ... then the reed.

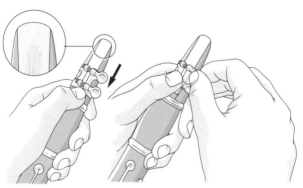

3 Check its position...   4 ... then tighten the ligature.

Better

If a reed feels too hard, set it a little lower down the mouthpiece. If it feels very light, try moving it up a bit, or try sliding the ligature down slightly, or loosening the upper screw a little. Reeds that are not perfectly even left and right will often perform better if you set them on your mouthpiece at a slight angle.

In line

Mouthpiece, upper and lower joints must all be in line.

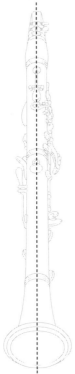

You can usually tell whether they are by looking at the brand name, if it is shown on all the sections. Alternatively, you can look along the underside of the instrument, from the bell to the reed. Some clarinets have special catches to make sure the upper and lower joints are always in line.

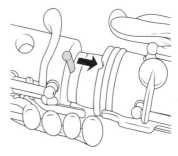

... a catch for the upper and lower joints...
(Leblanc)

Everything in line? Look along the underside of the instrument.

Brushing and flossing, food and drinks

If you want to make it as easy as possible to keep your clarinet clean, wash your hands and brush and floss your teeth before you play, don't eat during intermissions, and don't drink anything that contains sugar.

TUNING

Like every other instrument, a clarinet needs to be tuned before you start playing. The usual method of tuning is to pull the upper joint and barrel apart by some 0.04" to 0.08" (1–2 mm). A clarinet that sounds too low can only be tuned by using a shorter barrel.

Concert A   Tipcode CLR-016 and CLR-005

Most orchestras and bands tune to concert A (see page 37). On a B-flat clarinet that means you finger a B.

Tuning fork

If you have a piano or another keyboard instrument handy, you can sound concert A by playing the A just to the right of the center (A4). The same note will sound if you use a tuning fork in A. Just tap this small, thick fork against your knee, say, before setting the stem against your ear. Tuning forks are also available in other tunings (see pages 37–38). Electronic tuners and metronomes can often play this A too.

Tuning fork in A=440.

To other notes

In some groups it may be preferred to tune to other notes – the open G, for instance (concert F), or the D (concert C), because it is thought to be more stable than the B. Groups with many brass instruments (*e.g.*, concert bands and marching bands), most of which are pitched in B-flat, often tune to C (concert B-flat).

Barrel and upper joint

Quite often, tuning is simply a matter of pulling the barrel and upper joint apart slightly. However, that isn't always enough, because when you pull the barrel and upper joints apart, the short-tube notes go down further than the long-tube notes – just as they would when using a longer barrel (see page 70 and onwards).

The rest

If you also pull apart the upper and lower joints slightly, the notes that go down the most are the highest notes of the lower joint. By pulling out the bell a little, you can fine-tune the long-tube notes. If you are playing together with other clarinetists, it's usually best if you all tune in the same way.

Different notes

Because each clarinet has certain notes that tend to sound too low or too high, you should never tune to just one note. For instance, if you tune to an open G, you might try also playing the higher- and lower-sounding E and B (the notes of the E-minor chord) and listening to whether the distances between those notes are correct. If you are tuning to a C, you could also play the E and G (C-major chord).

Groove

When you pull two sections of a clarinet apart, a groove will be formed between them – on the outside, but also on the inside of the tube. This groove can cause the sound to deteriorate slightly. Moreover, condensation collects easily in the groove, and it increases the effects of tuning: When you pull the barrel out, the short-tune notes become even more obviously too low.

Tuning rings

The solution is to use *tuning rings*, which you place inside the tenons so that they fill up the groove. Tuning rings are usually sold in sets of two or three rings in various thicknesses (*i.e.*, 0.5, 1.0, and 2.0 mm), costing about five to ten dollars.

Some do, some don't

Some clarinets swear by tuning rings; other don't use them, because the rings need to be taken out if you want to tune to a higher pitch, or because they may start buzzing when you tune the clarinet a bit lower.

Tuners

An electronic tuner can be useful to tune your clarinet. Its built-in microphone 'hears' the note you are playing and tells you whether the pitch is sharp, flat or exactly right. A tip: You can get special tuners for transposing instruments, such as the clarinet. When you shift it to B-flat, the tuner will display a B-flat when you finger one, rather than the sounding pitch C. Another tip: Some tuners automatically switch off after a couple of minutes, which saves on batteries.

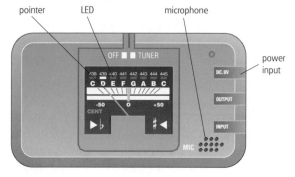

A chromatic tuner shows you which note it 'hears.'

Hotter means higher

After you've been playing for a while, your instrument will gradually warm up. This makes the tuning go up, so that after five to ten minutes' playing you'll often need to retune slightly. The better you warm up the instrument prior to playing, the less retuning will be necessary. Warming up your instrument is simply a matter of playing it, or blowing warm air through it, without making the reed vibrate.

AFTER

If you never clean your clarinet, the first thing you'll notice is that your mouthpiece starts smelling funny...

Reed

Reeds last longest if you rinse them and then dry them after playing (see page 82). If you leave your reed on the mouthpiece, it won't dry as easily, which will make it more likely to warp. Besides, you'll have to take it off to wet it next time you play anyway.

Reed cases

You can store the reed in a very basic open reed holder or in a reed guard, available for a couple of dollars, or get yourself a deluxe, leather-clad reed case for fifty dollars, or something in between.

Wet, dry...

Your reeds will dry most evenly in a reed case with ventilation holes and a ribbed floor, so that the air can get everywhere. Other cases have glass floors that help to prevent waves forming at the tip of the reed. What works best may depend on the reeds you use, and on how wet or dry they are when you store them. Some holders have replaceable cartridges containing a substance that keeps the humidity at the right level. Tip: Reeds can go moldy if you keep them in a case that's completely closed.

Numbered

Some reed cases and holders have numbered compartments, so you can tell the reeds apart. This is especially useful if you often change reeds or if you use different reeds for different situations.

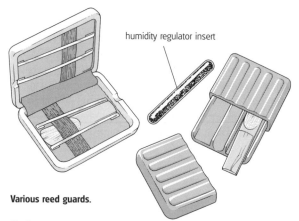

humidity regulator insert

Various reed guards.

Drying

Before you put your clarinet away, you need to dry it: That's better for the wood and for the pads. First, take the mouthpiece off and (ideally) rinse it in lukewarm water before you dry it, using a handkerchief or a special cloth.

Swabs
Tipcode CLR-017

Next dry the rest of the clarinet with a *swab*: a cloth with a cord and a weight attached to it. First lower the weight into the tube, then pull the cloth through the instrument.

From the bell upwards

The barrel is the part that gets the wettest, so it would seem logical to pull the cloth through the instrument from the bell upwards. All the same, some clarinetists prefer to do it the other way round (or both!), and some prefer to dry their instruments joint by joint. If you decide to do it that way, take the clarinet apart, lay the sections in the case, and take them out again one by one to dry them.

Caught

A swab can get caught behind the register tube or the thumbhole tube. Free it by pulling it back a little way in the other direction.

Tenons, toneholes, and pads

Don't forget to dry the tenons. Condensation often collects there, as it does in the toneholes. If you have wet toneholes, your pads won't make a proper seal. Sometimes you can dry toneholes simply by blowing on them from the outside. Otherwise, blow hard through the lower or upper joint. Dry wet pads with a cigarette paper (see pages 94–95).

Cotton or chamois

Most swabs have cotton cloths, but some have cloths made of chamois leather, silk, or wool. Cotton cloths need to be washed regularly, even when they are new: New cotton doesn't dry as well as old. Chamois, on the other hand, should not be washed.

Pad saver

Some clarinetists prefer to use a *pad saver*, a long fluffy plume that you stick into your clarinet after drying it. Others prefer not to, because pad savers leave behind fibers that can stick to the pads, because many don't absorb the moisture but spread it around, or because they may have metal rods that can damage the bore. Yet another alternative is a cloth-covered rod, which can be used to dry and clean the bore of the instrument.

Side pocket

The best place to keep your swab is in a side pocket of your case. If you store it in or with your clarinet, pads and springs can be affected by the moisture in the cloth.

Dry your clarinet with a pull-through swab.

Wait a while

If you can't easily take your clarinet apart after playing it, let it cool down for a while. If that doesn't help, don't use a wrench or undue force but wrap it in a towel (it will no longer fit inside its case) and take it to a technician.

Locked

Some cases have lids that automatically click shut when you close the case. If yours doesn't, always make sure you close the lid properly before you pick up the case. Too many clarinets have fallen out of unclosed cases.

AND IN BETWEEN

When you take a break, put the cap on the mouthpiece, and make sure your clarinet can't get damaged. It may be best to put the instrument on a clarinet stand. That way it will hardly take up any space. A clarinet stand also helps to prevent people from sitting down or stepping on your instrument.

Covered

You can buy a compactly folding clarinet stand for as little as ten to twenty dollars. The longer its feet are, the less chance there is that someone will knock it over. On some stands, the cone that the clarinet slides onto is covered with felt, which protects the bore against scratches and wear.

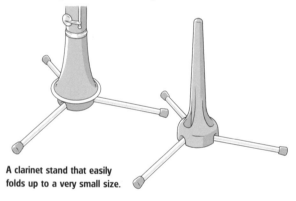

A clarinet stand that easily folds up to a very small size.

Don't

Never leave a clarinet where it will get too hot or too dry. Watch out for heaters, radiators, direct sunlight, air conditioning vents, and other dangerous spots.

Splutter

If you hear a spluttering sound at certain notes, it's probably down to moisture in a tonehole. The toneholes of the C-sharp/G-sharp key and the trill keys are especially sensitive to this problem, due to their position at the instrument: The moisture in the tube easily runs in their direction. Try to remove the moisture by blowing into the instrument real hard, or by blowing it off from the outside. Otherwise, slide a piece of *pad cleaning paper* or cigarette paper between the pad and the tonehole, so it can absorb the moisture. When using cigarette paper, make sure the gummed edge doesn't touch the pad. You can tear this edge off, but non-gummed cigarette papers are also available.

Oil
The pad of the C-sharp/G-sharp key is especially prone to becoming waterlogged. Some technicians prevent the problem by drawing a line of oil alongside or around the tonehole in question. The idea is that the moisture will follow the oil and not end up in the tonehole.

Sticky pads
Tipcode CLR-018

Sticky or damp pads – which you'll often find at the same keys – can be cleaned with pad cleaning paper or cigarette paper. Slide the paper under the pad, and hold the key closed for a little while. No improvement? Take a clean piece of paper, drip one or two drops of lighter fuel or an alcohol-based cleaning fluid onto it, and repeat the steps above. Dry the pad with a fresh piece of paper afterwards. Be careful when using lighter fuel or alcohol: both are highly flammable.

Preferably not
It's better not to clean or dry pads with talcum powder or other kinds of powder, banknotes, newspaper, or anything else with ink on it. If you have leather pads, you can use paper tissues to clean them.

Loose springs
If a key stops working, its spring may have come loose. Usually, it's quite easy to put it back into place. If the spring of a closed key is missing, you may be able to play on by holding the key shut with a rubber band. A tip: Take the rubber band off after playing and don't store any in your case. Rubber contains substances that are harmful to silver. Another tip: For the same reason, don't store erasers in your case.

Loose tenons
Sometimes the cork on one or several of the tenons is so

badly worn away that it doesn't grip or seal anymore. A temporary solution is to twist a cigarette paper or some yarn around it, but it's better to get the tenons recorked.

CASES AND BAGS

Most new clarinets come with their own case or bag, but these accessories are available separately too.

Five pieces

In most cases and bags you store your clarinet in five pieces: mouthpiece + cap + ligature as one, and then barrel, upper joint, lower joint, and bell. Others make you store it in two or three (very rarely), four (the bell stays on the lower joint) or more parts.

Hard-shell cases

Hard-shell cases usually have a molded plastic or plywood core and a plush lining. *French-style cases*, which have no handle, are often used in combination with a separate case cover in Cordura or a similar material. There are also hard-shell clarinet cases that look like a regular briefcase, hiding the fact that you are carrying a musical instrument.

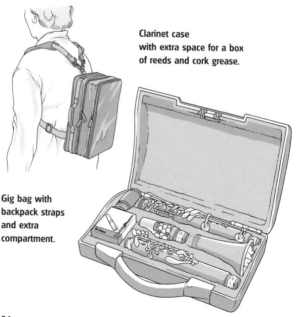

Clarinet case
with extra space for a box
of reeds and cork grease.

Gig bag with
backpack straps
and extra
compartment.

Bags

The same goes for so-called *carryall bags*, which have shoulder straps and lots of extra space that you can use for a music stand, sheet music, and other bits and pieces. *Gig bags* are soft 'cases' with thickly-lined sides. They usually come with an accessory pocket, a sheet music compartment, and adjustable backpack straps that offer a safe way to transport a clarinet when biking or walking.

Space

If you are buying a new case or bag, check how much extra storage space it offers. Will you be able to fit a box of reeds and a reed guard in it, or a second mouthpiece, an extra barrel, cork grease, or a neck strap? Does it have a side pocket for your swab, a music stand, a lyre, or sheet music?

Prices

Cases and bags are on sale from around forty dollars. If you want a luxury version, with a wooden shell, leather covering, and space for two clarinets (*e.g.*, A and B-flat), you can easily spend ten times that amount.

EXTRAS

A few odds and ends at the end of this chapter: lyres for marching clarinetists, microphones for clarinetists who need to go louder, and travel tips for everyone.

Lyre

Marching clarinetists put their sheet music on a *lyre*, which will fit on the instrument without the use of drills or

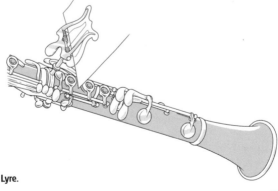

Lyre.

screws. Some lyres offer a separate attachment point for a neck strap. Most lyres are designed to be attached half way up the clarinet. Lyres that are attached at the bell make it harder to read the music.

Louder

If your clarinet needs to be amplified occasionally, you can use a good vocal microphone. If it happens more often, you may consider a special clarinet miking system. These systems often feature two small microphones to capture the sound which emerges from the entire instrument, rather than just from the bell.

Preamplifier

The microphones are attached to the instrument. Because the mics only produce a very weak signal, they come with a separate preamplifier, which you can either put in your pocket or attach to your clothing. The preamp, which usually allows you to control volume and tone (bass/treble), sends the signal to the power amplifier.

Movement or variation

These dedicated systems give you more freedom to move around than a microphone on a stand, without changing sound or volume. On the other hand, if your microphone is on a stand, you can deliberately influence volume and tone by changing the distance between the mic and your instrument.

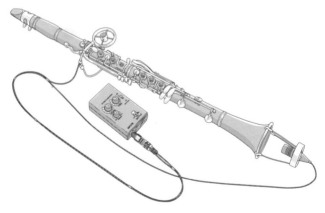

A clarinet with two dedicated clip-on microphones (SD Systems).

On the road

- Don't put a clarinet **on the luggage shelf of a car**, under the rear window – especially not on a hot day.
- Getting **out of the car**? Always take your instrument with you.
- All kinds of things – including clarinets – get left behind in the **luggage racks** of buses, trains, and subways. Tip: Keep hold of your instrument.
- Consider **insuring your instrument**, especially if you take it on the road – which includes visiting your teacher. Musical instruments fall under the insurance category of 'valuables.' A regular homeowners' insurance policy will usually not cover all possible damage, whether it occurs at home, on the road, in the studio, or onstage.
- To get your instrument insured you'll need to know the **serial number** and some other details. There is space for that information on pages 132–133. Insurance companies also often ask for an appraisal report (see page 25) and proof of purchase.

9. MAINTENANCE

If you always do everything you read in the previous chapter, your clarinet probably won't need much additional maintenance. A bit of extra cleaning now and again, and perhaps the odd drop of oil – that's all there is to it. Once in a while, though, you will need to take your clarinet to a technician for a COA (cleaning, oiling, and adjustment) or an overhaul.

Ebonite mouthpieces should be cleaned now and then, preferably in lukewarm water. A special mouthpiece brush is useful. Remove chalk scale with a mouthpiece cleaner, which will also disinfect the mouthpiece.

Water

Don't leave ebonite and wooden mouthpieces to soak in water, and avoid using vinegar or liquid soap if you want to keep them looking their best. Vinegar and liquid soap won't damage most other types of mouthpieces, though.

Polishing the keywork

A nickel-plated mechanism needs no more than a shine with a dry cloth. If you have a silver-plated mechanism, you can use a silver polishing cloth to clean it and restore its luster. Don't use it too often, though: The built-in polishing agent will eventually wear through the plating.

No ordinary polish

Ordinary silver and metal polishes tend to be too abrasive for musical instruments: They can damage your pads, and residue may get into the hinges, gumming up the keywork. To be avoided, in other words.

Black

If your silver-plated keywork tarnishes faster than you can polish it (see page 41), you're better off getting an instrument with a nickel-plated mechanism, or having the mechanism gold-plated. A sudden discoloration of the keywork can be caused by something in your diet, such as spinach or eggs, certain medicines, erasers or rubber bands in your case, or even a new ebonite mouthpiece. If your mouthpiece seems to be the guilty party, store it in a plastic bag outside the case for the first few weeks.

Oiling the mechanism

The best way to oil the mechanism is to take it apart completely – so it's best to leave this to a technician. If only a few of the keys need to be lubricated, and you decide to do it yourself, use as little oil as possible. First dip a match or a pin into a little oil on a saucer or a piece of paper; then apply it to the hinge. Buy special clarinet key oil from your music store, not whatever you happen to have at home. Two tips: Oil is disastrous for pads, and don't oil a mechanism that already works smoothly.

Cleaning

The best way to clean the little nooks and crannies of the mechanism is with a small brush. The more often you do this, the less chance that dust and dirt will lodge there.

Wobble

When you're polishing the mechanism, check for wobble too. Wobble (backlash) may simply be down to a loose screw, but it can also be caused by wear. A tip: Get your clarinet checked by a technician: If you don't, it'll get worse.

Toneholes

Even if you always play with clean hands, the edges of the open toneholes will eventually become dirty. There are special cleaning sticks available. Q-Tips will do too, as long as you make sure that the cotton fibers don't end up in the keywork or the instrument.

Rings

Now and then, check whether the bell ring, tenon rings, and body rings are still tight. Loose rings can cause buzzes.

They also show that the wood has shrunk, indicating that the clarinet has been stored in conditions that are too dry. Air conditioning and central heating systems are two of the main causes of dry air. An air humidity level of 40 to 60 percent is usually considered good for both musical instruments and human beings.

OILING THE BORE

There are few things clarinetists disagree about as strongly as oiling the bores of wooden clarinets. Some do it every three months, while others haven't used oil for decades – and never had problems. Some factories recommend that you oil a new clarinet, others advise against it. The simplest tip? Ask for advice when you buy your instrument, or leave it to your technician.

Cracks

Most experts believe that a thin film of oil in the bore reduces the risk of cracks. Others say that grenadilla is so hard and strong that oil could never prevent a clarinet from cracking. The only thing that can be said for sure is that wooden clarinets sometimes crack, whether or not they have been frequently oiled.

The best way

Oil hardly penetrates the wood, if at all, but leaves behind a thin, protective film. The best way to oil the bore is to first allow the instrument to dry thoroughly. Then remove the mechanism, oil the wood, clean the toneholes, reassemble the instrument, and adjust it – a job for a professional, in other words.

Easier

The easiest way to oil the bore is to dry the instrument as well as you can, put pieces of cling film under all the pads, put a very small amount of oil on a special cleaning rod, and move it backwards and forwards through the tube a few times. An important tip: It's easier to damage a clarinet by using too much oil than by using too little.

Almond oil and bore oil

There are special bore oils for sale, and sweet almond oil is often used as well. These types of oil don't dry, which means they easily get wiped off and you would have to use them quite often.

Hard oil or wax

Linseed oil and tung oil do dry, so they stay on longer. These 'hard' oil types are best applied by an expert. Why? For one thing, if you use a bit too much you can end up with a crusty, gel-like layer inside your clarinet… Rather than oil, some players use beeswax.

SERVICE AND OVERHAULS

New clarinets need to be checked and adjusted after six months to a year. In some cases, that first service is included in the purchase price.

Cleaning, oiling, and adjusting

If you get your clarinet checked once a year, you can be fairly sure that nothing major can go wrong. Some technicians consider once every two years to be sufficient, depending on how much you play. Expect to pay some fifty to seventy-five dollars for an annual checkup or COA (cleaning, oiling, adjusting). The longer you wait, the more expensive it can get.

Overhaul

Clarinets need to be overhauled once every five to ten years. If you choose, you can have your instrument made as good as new, with new pads, new tenons, new silver-plating, new springs, new rods, and new screws… The price will depend on what needs to be done, but also on the quality and age of the clarinet.

Try it out

Whether you take your instrument for a COA or a full overhaul, it will be adjusted. A tip: Try your instrument out before you take it home again, so that you know that it plays the way you want it to. Adjustment is a very personal thing, after all. On the other hand: You may have to get used to the instrument feeling differently, especially if the adjustment was way off.

10. BACK IN TIME

If you read ten books on the history of the clarinet, chances are each will tell a different story – and no one knows who's right. Everybody does agree, however, that the earliest predecessors of the instrument date back some five thousand years, and that the clarinet itself is about three hundred years of age.

To find the very first predecessors of the clarinet you have to go back at least until ancient Egypt, where they were playing the *memet* as long ago as 3000 BC.

Idioglottic

The memet had an *integral reed*: The reed is cut from the tube itself, staying attached to it at one end only. This makes the memet an *idioglottic instrument*.

One tube or two

The clarinet had many other ancestors and early family members, such as the Greek *aulos*, the Chinese *cuen kan*, the ancient Arabian *arghul*, and the Welsh *pibcorn* or *hornpipe*: All instruments with a single reed, many with one tube, some with two.

Chalumeau

The chalumeau was another single-reed instrument. According to some experts, the chalumeau was first played two thousand years ago; others regard the Middle Ages as more likely. Some expert books will tell you that not a single chalumeau has been preserved, while other, equally scholarly works show photographs of the instrument…

Register key

The most important difference between the chalumeau and the first clarinets is the register key. Missing this key, the chalumeau had a range no larger than – of course – the chalumeau register of the modern clarinet.

Clarinet

With the introduction of the register key the range of the instrument was extended considerably. The new, higher register in some ways resembled the sound of a trumpet, and so the clarinet got its name; the word clarinet is derived from the Italian word for trumpet, *clarino*, or small trumpet, *clarinetto*.

Denner and Sons

It is unclear who exactly invented the register key, and hence the clarinet. Most sources do agree that the inventor was called Denner. Some experts claim it was the Nuremberg instrument maker Johann Christian Denner; others say it must have been one of his sons, because the clarinet is first mentioned in 1710, three years after the death of Denner Senior.

Five to six keys

Gradually, the clarinet acquired more keys: Without those extra keys, you would only be able to play it in a few different key signatures. Around 1800, most clarinets had around five or six keys.

Iwan Müller

In 1812, the clarinetist Iwan Müller produced a clarinet with thirteen keys, enough to play it in any key signature.

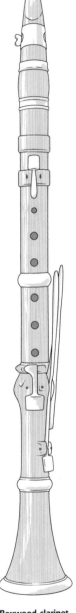

Boxwood clarinet in C with five keys and ivory body rings
(Savary, Paris, 1780; collection Jac. Schaap).

Those thirteen keys were not the only ace up Müller's sleeve: He also used a metal ligature, and was one of the first clarinetists to turn the mouthpiece around. Before then, the instrument was played with the reed facing upwards.

Bärmann and Oehler

Half a century later, Carl Bärmann added a further five or six keys to the Müller clarinet, and another half a century after that, Oskar Oehler used Bärmann's design as the basis for his own clarinet system, which most German professionals still play today.

Albert and Sax

Improvements on Müller's work were being made in Belgium, too, by among others Eugène Albert, after whom the 'German' Albert system is named. Another famous Belgian who occupied himself with the clarinet was Adolphe Sax, who invented the 'sax-o-phone' around 1840.

Klosé and Buffet

Around the same time, the Frenchmen Hyacinte Klosé and Louis Auguste Buffet were also working on the clarinet. Put simply, they took some of the ideas of Theobald Boehm, the inventor of the modern (Boehm) flute, and applied them to the clarinet. Boehm himself had nothing else to do with their clarinet, but the instrument was nevertheless named after him.

Perfect, or not?

Since Albert, Oehler, and the first Boehm clarinets, nothing much has changed. Some experts say that is a good thing, since they consider the modern clarinet to be a perfect instrument. Others feel the clarinet is still in its infancy stage, because there's so much left to be improved…

11. THE FAMILY

The immediate clarinet family consists of at least thirteen clarinets in different tunings. All kinds of other instruments with single reeds are also related, and if you include all the members of the woodwind family of instruments, you need to add the saxophone, the flute, the oboe, and others besides.

Clarinets come in all kinds of tunings. The most popular is of course the soprano clarinet in B-flat, followed by the soprano clarinets in A (slightly larger, and lower in pitch) and E-flat (shorter, and higher), and there are also sopranos in C and D. The E-flat instrument is so much smaller that it often doesn't have separate upper and lower joints.

A few in A-flat and C
Smaller still, and much rarer, are the sopranino clarinets. There are two of them: in A-flat and in C.

Basset clarinet
The *basset clarinet* is an extended soprano clarinet in A. Because of the extra length the lowest note is a C, instead of the usual E. The basset clarinet is often used for Mozart's famous clarinet concerto – which is why it is sometimes known as a *Mozart clarinet*.

Basset horn
The modern *basset horn*, pitched in F, most closely resembles an alto clarinet. The German version has the basset keys, which are operated with the right thumb, at the back of the instrument, while the French version has them

at the front. Earlier basset horns came in many different models; one of them had a semi-circular tube, which explains the 'horn' part of its name.

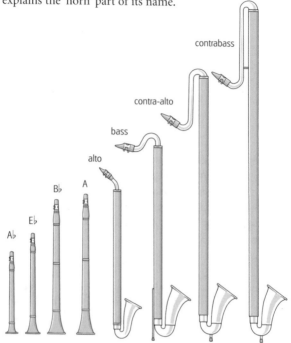

All the clarinet sizes side by side.

Contra-alto, contrabass, and sub-contrabass

If you want to go lower still, you need a *contra-alto clarinet* in EE-flat or a *contrabass clarinet* in BB-flat, sounding an octave lower than the alto clarinet and the bass clarinet respectively. Both come in various models, some featuring a straight wooden, metal or plastic tube, others a coiled metal tube with two bows in it. The curves make these long instruments a bit shorter, so you don't need to stand up to play them. Finally, there's the extremely rare *sub-contrabass clarinet*, which sounds another octave lower than the contrabass.

Harmony clarinets

All clarinets larger or smaller than the soprano are often collectively called *harmony clarinets*. In many orchestras and ensembles they are used to play the harmonies that accompany the soloist or the melody.

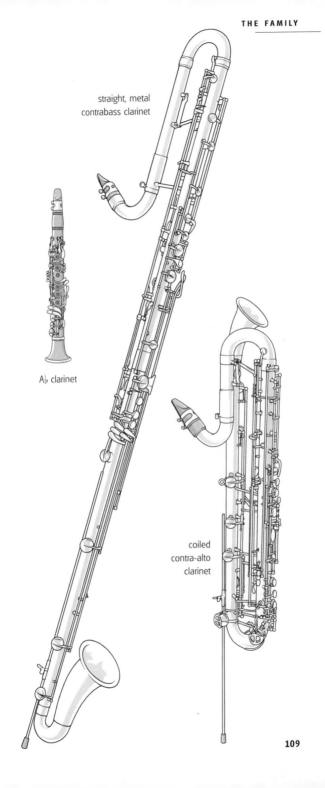

straight, metal
contrabass clarinet

A♭ clarinet

coiled
contra-alto
clarinet

Turkish and Greek in G

There are many other varieties of clarinet – for instance, the metal soprano clarinet in G, which is much used in Turkish and Greek music.

Folk clarinets

Besides the members of the immediate clarinet family, closely related instruments can be found in various countries and cultures. The most important thing they have in common is that they all have single reeds. Most of them have only five or six toneholes, and no keys. One of the best known is the wooden Hungarian *tárogató*, which most closely resembles a widely-flared clarinet, or, depending on how you look at it, a wooden soprano saxophone.

WOODWIND INSTRUMENTS

The clarinet belongs to the family of woodwind instruments, as do the saxophone, the flute, the oboe, and the bassoon, among others.

Saxophone   Tipcode CLR-019

The saxophone is perhaps the instrument that is closest to the clarinet. Both the mouthpiece and the mechanism are very similar.

Conical

Two major differences are that saxophones have a brass body, which becomes steadily wider from the mouthpiece onwards. This makes it sound and play quite differently. If you open the register key or *octave key* of a saxophone, it sounds an octave higher.

Flute   Tipcode CLR-019

If you look only at the keywork, a flute looks a lot like a clarinet too. This is not surprising: The Boehm clarinet mechanism is derived from the mechanism that Theobald Boehm invented for the flute.

Air stream

The flute has no register key. You move up to a higher register by varying your air stream, a technique known as *overblowing*. When you overblow, you go up an octave.

A flute, an oboe, an alto saxophone, and a soprano saxophone.

Oboe
Tipcode CLR-019

Oboes have a conical body, like saxophones, and they're made of wood, like clarinets. Even so, the oboe sounds very different from both instruments, mainly because it has a different type of reed: An oboe is a *double-reed instrument*. The sound is created by two reeds vibrating against each other, as is the sound of the much larger bassoon.

STOPPED PIPE

Why is the clarinet the only woodwind instrument that goes up a twelfth when you change register, rather than an octave, like the other woodwinds? Because it has a (largely) cylindrical tube, which is blocked at one end – by the mouthpiece. As a result, a clarinet acoustically behaves like a *stopped pipe*.

Three times as fast

In a stopped pipe, going up to the next register makes the air vibrate three times as fast. An example: If you play a concert E3, the air vibrates 165 times a second (165Hz). If you then go to the next higher register, the air vibrates three times as fast, at 495Hz, producing a concert B4.

Much lower

Stopped pipes sound a lot lower than you would expect from their length. For instance, a clarinet sounds almost an octave lower than a soprano saxophone, a flute, and an oboe, although all four instruments are pretty much the same length.

Open or conical

In other words, flutes, oboes, and saxophones don't behave like stopped pipes – flutes because they are open at both ends, and saxophones and oboes because they have conical instead of cylindrical bores. If you move up to the next register on these instruments, the air starts vibrating twice as fast, which makes the pitch an octave higher.

12. HOW THEY'RE MADE

There are all kinds of larger and smaller differences between the ways cheaper and more expensive clarinets are made.

The material for wooden clarinets is delivered to the factory as square-ended blocks or billets: longer ones for the upper and lower joints, short ones for the barrels and big, almost square blocks for the bells. In order to prevent the wood from cracking later, it first needs to be thoroughly dried and cured. Before the drying process, the square blocks are turned on a lathe to cut them into a round shape, after which a hole is drilled down the middle lengthways. This will later become the bore.

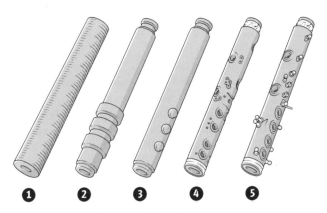

A lower joint in various stages of manufacture:
Pre-drilled, roughly turned and dried (1), more finely machined, with bands for the integral toneholes and with tenons (2), with chimneys (3), toneholes and holes for the mechanism drilled (4), and with posts (5).

Years or hours

The wood is sometimes still left to dry for years, in the old-fashioned way. However, in most factories this stage takes place in special kilns, which dry the wood much faster. More expensive clarinets are often made of older wood, which has the least risk of cracking.

Cut and drilled
Tipcode CLR-020

After drying, the sections are shaped with a variety of drills and lathes, which are usually computer-controlled. As the outside is lathed, the upper and lower joints for instruments with integral toneholes (see page 36) are left with raised bands of wood on the outside, as the illustration shows.

Molds

The sections of plastic clarinets are often molded: The material is poured into a mold, and when it comes out it basically has its final shape.

Polishing

The wooden sections are extensively polished to make them mirror-smooth and shiny. Often they are then submerged in an oil bath for several days or even longer. To make colored instruments, the oil may be mixed with East India ink, for example.

Posts and mechanism

Once all the sections are ready, the posts and rings are attached, and the keywork is mounted and adjusted.

Testing and fine-tuning

Before they leave the factory, instruments are usually play-tested. The more expensive the clarinet, the more attention will usually be devoted to the final testing and adjusting stage. High-end instruments may also be fine-tuned by hand, for example by very carefully reworking the toneholes and the bore.

REEDS AND MOUTHPIECES

Most reeds are made of *Arundo donax*, a type of cane that grows particularly well in Var in southern France, but also in South America, Australia, and elsewhere.

Curing

The plants are harvested when they are two to three years old. By then they have usually grown to about 25 feet (8 meters). After harvesting, the cane is first allowed to dry for a year or more, during which time it cures and develops its golden yellow color.

By size and into shape
Tipcode CLR-021

The tubes are chopped into short pieces and then sorted by size: larger ones for the big reeds used on bass clarinets or large saxophones, smaller ones for small E-flat clarinets, and so on. Afterwards, each tube is usually split into four pieces, the quarters being cut and shaped further by a whole series of machines: The reed is flattened, the facing polished, the profile made and the tip cut into its round shape. At each stage, the reeds are inspected visually, discarding the bad ones.

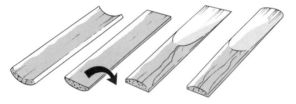

From cane to reed in four steps.

Number

A special device measures the resistance of each reed at the tip. The higher the resistance, the harder the reed, and the higher the number it is given. Next, the reeds are once again inspected thoroughly, stamped, and packed.

Mouthpieces

Most mouthpieces start life as small blocks of ebonite, glass, wood or metal, which are cut into shape by computer-controlled lathes. On more expensive mouthpieces, the shape of the facing is still finished by hand. The very cheapest plastic mouthpieces are cast in one go.

13. BRANDS

When taking a look at some of the main brand names in the clarinet industry, the French heritage of the instrument is quite clear, with four of the larger companies stemming from that country. Yet clarinets are being made all over the world.

**Artley®** Donald Artley started out as a flute maker in the early 1900s. The first clarinets were made in the 1960s. The American company focuses on beginners' and student clarinets, and also makes other woodwinds.

Buffet-Crampon was formed when Jean Louis Buffet married Zoé Crampon in 1836. The French company makes clarinets in all price ranges, as well oboes and saxophones. The cheaper clarinet series come from the German company Schreiber.

®Leblanc Leblanc is the best-known brand of the company that also owns the brands Vito, Noblet, and Holton. The Leblanc brand name is used for French-made wooden clarinets in all price ranges, while plastic US-made clarinets are sold under the Vito and Holton brand names. Noblet clarinets are made in France.

* Trademarks and/or usernames have been used in this book solely to identify the products or instruments discussed. Such use does not identify endorsement by or affiliation with the trademark owner(s).

Henri Selmer, solo clarinetist with the Paris Opéra Comique, started his company in 1885. The French Selmer company makes all the popular sizes in the clarinet family, both in the professional and the mid-price ranges, as well as saxophones and trumpets.

Selmer® The American Selmer company, which has a different owner than its French namesake, evolved from the collaboration of Selmer France and the American company Buesscher in the early 1900s. Selmer USA makes student and intermediate clarinets in wood and plastic.

YAMAHA® The one-man organ factory founded by Torakusu Yamaha in 1889 is now the world's biggest producer of musical instruments, from clarinets to guitars and from synthesizers to pianos and the Japanese company also makes motorbikes, hi-fi equipment, and much more.

AND BESIDES

A few other brand names you may come across include **Armstrong** (American; mainly known for its flutes), **Ridenour** (American; synthetic clarinets), **Amati** (Czech maker of a wide variety of wind instruments, and one of the few to still build full-boehm clarinets; see page 45), the Taiwanese **Dixon** and **Jupiter** brands, which also make other (wind) instruments, **Orsi** and **Ripamonti** from Italy, and **Lark** from China. These brands are mainly active in the lower price range.

Higher

Some other brands focus especially on the higher price ranges, such as **Eaton**, **Hanson**, and **Howarth** (UK), the Italian firm **Patricola**, and the Chilean company **Rossi**, whose products include one-piece B-flat clarinets.

GERMAN CLARINETS

Most German factories either largely or exclusively make clarinets with the German or Oehler system. A few of the better-known names are **Bernd Moosman**, **Richard Keilwerth**, **Arthur Uebel**, **Püchner**, **Schwenk & Seggelke**, and **Schreiber**, which collaborates with Buffet-Crampon, and **Hammerschmidt**, which also makes Austrian clarinets, tárogatós, and other woodwind instruments. The best known German brand name, to be found on very expensive clarinets only, is that of **Herbert Wurlitzer**. The clarinets made by Herbert's father and predecessor **Fritz Wurlitze**r are at least as celebrated.

OLD BRAND NAMES

On older clarinets you may sometimes come across brand names from the past. One example is **Bundy**, a brand name you'll find on many secondhand beginners' instruments. Two European examples are the French brand **SML** (Strasser-Marigaux-Lemaire), also known as **Marigaux**, which was discontinued in the late 1990s, and **Boosey & Hawkes**, the British company that stopped making its own clarinets when it bought Buffet-Crampon, mentioned above.

14. GROUPS AND ORCHESTRAS

Clarinetists play in concert bands, clarinet choirs, wind quintets, duos, trios, gypsy orchestras, Dixieland groups, jazz bands, symphony orchestras, and all kinds of other groups and ensembles. Here's an introduction to some of those groups, the music they play and what role clarinetists play in them.

The clarinet is the most important instrument in a concert band. These large orchestras, often made up of between about forty and a hundred musicians, may play various styles of music, from classical to modern. The role of the B-flat clarinets can often be compared to that of the violins in a symphony orchestra. Besides a large number of B-flat clarinetists, concert bands also have E-flat, alto, and bass clarinetists, and sometimes bigger and smaller clarinets are also used.

Other instruments
Furthermore, a concert band has a brasswind section (trumpet, trombone, and so on), a percussion section, there are other woodwind players (saxes and flutes), and there may be other instruments as well.

Marching bands
A marching band is composed mainly of wind players and percussionists, who perform while marching, either onstage, in parades, or during football games.

Symphony orchestras
The violin usually plays the leading role in the symphony

orchestra, as the clarinet often does in concert bands. Most symphony orchestras have two to four clarinetists, just about always on B-flat and A clarinet: Many classical works for symphony orchestras require both instruments. One or two of the clarinetists usually play the E-flat clarinet too, and often there is a separate bass clarinet player. A symphony orchestra also includes other woodwind instruments, a brass section, other strings (viola, cello, double bass), percussion, and other instruments.

Smaller classical

Classical music can be played in smaller ensembles too. Chamber orchestras, for instance, which have around twenty to forty musicians, or even smaller groups. For example, music has been written for duos (two clarinets), wind trios (clarinet, bassoon, and French horn), wind quartets (plus oboe) and wind quintets (plus flute), sometimes accompanied by a piano, and for all kinds of different line-ups.

With strings

Clarinetists often play together with strings, too: Their sounds blend particularly well. Special works have been written for clarinet/string combinations. Alternatively, the clarinet can take the place of one of the violins in a string quartet. That means playing with a second violinist, a viola player, and a cellist. Indeed, an alto clarinet could take over the part of the viola, and a bass clarinet replace the cello.

Solo

Clarinetists can also perform as soloists, just like violinists, pianists, and other musicians. For example, plenty of music has been written for clarinet and orchestra.

Modern classical

Classical music is not just 'old' music, as is often thought. It's still being written today too. Some composers specialize in contemporary or avant-garde music, often using all kinds of unusual sounds and special effects and techniques in their works.

The bass clarinet is especially prominent in this type of music, because the instrument offers a lot of scope for experimentation with unusual sounds.

CLARINET CHOIRS

More and more groups are being formed that consist entirely of clarinetists. These clarinet choirs may have five, fifteen, fifty, or even more musicians.

All levels, all styles

Clarinet choirs exist at different levels, from amateur to professional, and may play all kinds of styles: hits, international folk music, works specially written for clarinet choirs, arrangements of works for concert bands and symphony orchestras, and much more besides.

From large to small

The bigger a clarinet choir is, the more likely it will be to have a conductor. The B-flat clarinetists are always the biggest group. All kinds of other clarinets may be used in addition, from the tiny A-flat sopranino to the contrabass.

AND MORE

Apart from that, you can play all kinds of other styles as a clarinetist, in a wide variety of groups. Clarinets are used in the folk music of many different countries and regions (the Czech Republic, the Balkans, Turkey and Greece, for example), as they are in gypsy and klezmer orchestras, in world music bands, and in groups that accompany vocalists, choirs, or musicals.

Jazz

No Dixieland band is complete without a clarinetist, and you often find the instrument in big bands too. The saxophone edged out the clarinet in jazz in the 1940s, but in recent years the clarinet has once again been slowly gaining ground, often as a second instrument played by saxophonists.

Jazz and classical

The versatility of the clarinet is shown especially by the many great clarinetists who have become famous by playing jazz while being equally at home playing classical works – from Benny Goodman, Woody Herman, and Eric Dolphy in the past to Eddie Daniels and Don Byron today.

GLOSSARY AND INDEX

This glossary contains short definitions of all the clarinet-related terms used in this book. There are also some words you won't find in the previous pages, but which you might well come across in magazines, catalogs, and books. The numbers refer to the pages where the terms are used in this book.

12th key If you open the *12th key* or *register key* of a clarinet, the note you are playing goes up by a twelfth, taking you to the next register. See also: *Register, register key.*

17/6 *(7)* Most clarinets have seventeen keys and six rings.

A clarinet *(48)* Sounds a half-tone (half-step) lower than the B-flat clarinet.

Acute register See: *Register, register key.*

Albert clarinet See: *German clarinet.*

Altissimo register See: *Register, register key.*

Alto clarinet *(12–13, 33)* Is slightly larger than a B-flat clarinet; it sounds slightly lower.

Articulated G-sharp *(45)* Extra key that makes various trills easier to play.

Auxiliary E-flat lever *(44)* An extra lever that allows you to operate the A-flat/E-flat key with your left little finger, as well as with the right one.

Baffle *(61, 67)* A baffle lowers the palate of the mouthpiece, making the sound brighter and more direct.

Barrel *(4, 5, 29, 54, 70–72)*

Joint that connects the mouthpiece and the upper joint. Also known as *tuning barrel* and *socket*.

Bass clarinet *(2, 12–13, 30, 47, 120)* Sounds an octave lower than a soprano clarinet in B-flat.

Bell *(5, 29, 33–34)* The widely flared end of the clarinet.

B-flat clarinet *(3, 11)* The most popular clarinet is the soprano clarinet in B-flat: the C fingering sounds a concert B-flat.

Boehm clarinet *(14, 49, 51)* The Boehm clarinet or French clarinet is the most popular type of clarinet.

Bore *(30–33, 49–50, 57)* The dimensions and shape of the inside of the instrument. Most important 'component' of the clarinet, along with the bore of the mouthpiece *(67–68)* and the barrel *(72)*.

Break register See: *Register, register key.*

Bridge *(10–11, 86)* The connection between the upper joint and the lower joint. Also called *bridge mechanism* or *connection*, or *correspondence*.

Chalumeau 1. See: *Register, register key.* 2. Forefather of the clarinet *(104)*.

Chamber *(61, 62, 67)* The internal space of a mouthpiece.

Clarinet register, clarino register, clarion register See: *Register, register key.*

Closed-hole keys *(13, 16, 51)* Keys with solid key cups rather than rings. Also known as *plateau-style keys.*

Connection See: *Bridge.*

Dalbergia melanoxylon See: *Grenadilla.*

Double cut See: *French file cut.*

E-flat clarinet *(12, 13, 22, 107)* A smaller, higher-sounding clarinet.

Embouchure *(15)* The way you use your lips, jaws, tongue, and all the muscles around them when playing a wind instrument.

Facing, facing length *(61–62, 64, 66–67)* The term 'facing' may describe the tip opening of a mouthpiece, the lay (curvature, length, or both). See also: *Lay.* The term is also used for the underside of a reed.

File cut See: *French file cut.*

Fork B-flat *(44)* An extra ring, offering an alternative (fork) fingering for B-flat.

French clarinet Another name for the Boehm clarinet. See: *Boehm clarinet.*

French file cut *(77)* A reed with a *French file cut* has an extra section at the end of the thick part filed away in a straight line. Also known as *file cut*, *French cut*, or *double cut*, as opposed to reeds with a *single cut*.

Full-Boehm *(45)* A rare clarinet with many extra keys and options.

German clarinet *(48–52, 63, 69–70, 106)* German clarinets have a different bore and a different mechanism, mouthpiece, and reed from French or Boehm clarinets. There are various systems, such as the German or Albert system, and the Oehler system. Reform-Boehm clarinets *(51)* have a German bore and a French mechanism. See also: *Boehm clarinet.*

Grenadilla *(29)* The most commonly used type of wood for clarinets. Also known as ebony, m'pingo or African blackwood,

officially called *Dalbergia melanoxylon.*

Insurance *(99, 132)* Smart move.

Integral toneholes See: *Toneholes.*

Intonation *(52–54)* The better the intonation of a clarinet is, the easier it is to play in tune.

Key cups The actual 'lids' that stop the tone holes. Also known as *pad cups.*

Key opening See: *Venting.*

Keys *(4–5, 7, 10–11, 42–47, 58–59)* A clarinet has keys with pads, and open *rings* or *ring keys.*

Keywork See: *Mechanism.*

Klosé clarinet *(106)* Another name for the French or Boehm clarinet, invented by Hyacinte Klosé.

Lay *(62)* The area where the mouthpiece curves away from the reed, from the tip of the reed to the point where the reed touches the mouthpiece. See also: *Facing, facing length.*

Ligature *(4, 5, 73–74)* A clamp that attaches your reed to your mouthpiece.

Long-pipe notes, long-tube notes *(33, 57)* The notes you play with most or all of the keys closed, so that you are using a long section of the clarinet tube. When all or most of the keys are open, you play *short-pipe notes* or *short-tube notes*.

Lyre *(97)* Holder for sheet music, to be mounted onto the instrument.

M'pingo See: *Grenadilla*.

Mechanism *(38–47)* The entire system of keys and rods that allow you to open and close all the toneholes. Also called the *keywork* or *key system*.

Mode See: *Register, register key*.

Mouthpiece *(4–5, 54, 59, 60–70, 115)* How you sound and play depends primarily on your mouthpiece and your reed.

Mouthpiece cushion *(69)* A thin cushion that protects both the mouthpiece and your teeth.

Neck *(72–73)* Alto, bass, and other large clarinets have a metal neck instead of a barrel. Also known as *crook*.

Neck strap *(16)* Takes the weight of the instrument off your thumb.

Nickel-plated See: *Silver-plated*.

Octave key See: *Register key*.

Oehler clarinet See: *German clarinet*.

Pad cups See: *Key cups*.

Pads *(11, 47–48, 58, 92, 94–95)* Small discs made of felt or cork, covered in animal membrane, leather, or plastic, which seal the toneholes.

Plateau-style keys See: *Closed-hole keys*.

Posts *(41)* The metal pillars by which the mechanism is attached to the clarinet.

Power-forged keys *(42)* Keys that are shaped by pressure, rather than cast.

Rails *(66–67)* The tip rail and the side rails are the three edges of the window of a mouthpiece.

Reed *(4–5, 63, 75–83, 87, 91, 114–115)* Comparable to a string when you play the guitar or your vocal cords when you sing.

Reed cutter *(81)* Tool used

to slightly shorten reeds that are too light.

Reed guard *(91–92)* Protective holder for reeds.

Reform-Boehm See: *German clarinet.*

Register, register key *(7–10, 47, 50, 52–53, 110–112)* The register key allows you to move from the low *chalumeau register* to the *clarinet register* (also known as *clarion register, clarino register, upper register* or *overblown register*). The third and highest register is called the *acute register,* the *altissimo register,* or the *aigu register.* The register key is also known as the *speaker key, 12th key* or, wrongly, the *octave key.* The four highest notes of the chalumeau register (G – B-flat) are indicated as the *break* or *throat register (58).* The registers are also referred to as *modes.*

Register tube *(36–37)* Small tube attached to the register key tonehole; also known as *speaker tube.*

Rings, ring keys See: *Keys.*

Second-hand buying tips *(24–25, 58–59)*

Short-pipe notes, short-

tube notes See: *Long-pipe notes, long-tube notes.*

Silver-plated *(41, 100–101)* Clarinets either have silver-plated or nickel-plated mechanisms.

Single cut See: *French file cut.*

Single-reed instruments *(104, 111)* Clarinets are single-reed instruments, as are saxophones.

Socket See: *Barrel.*

Soprano clarinet *(3, 107)* The most popular clarinet is the soprano clarinet in B-flat. There are other soprano clarinets in A, C, D and E-flat.

Speaker key See: *Register, register key.*

Speaker tube See: *Register tube.*

Stopped pipe *(111–112)* A cylindrical instrument which is blocked at one end acoustically behaves like a stopped pipe. The clarinet belongs to this group.

Throat register See: *Register, register key.*

Thumb key See: *Register, register key.*

Thumb rest *(5, 40)* Helps support the instrument.

Tip opening *(61–62, 65–66)* The distance between the tip of your reed and the tip of your mouthpiece. See also: *Facing, facing length.*

Toneholes *(4, 35–38)* The holes in your clarinet. They are often undercut, which means that each hole gets slightly wider at the bottom. Integral toneholes are explained on pages 36 and 114.

Transposing *(12)* Clarinets are transposing instruments: The fingering you play has a different name from the tone you hear. The only exceptions are C clarinets.

Trill keys *(42)* Only the upper two of the four keys that you play with the side of your right hand index finger are actually designed for playing trills, but often all of them are referred to as *trill keys.*

Tuning *(37–38, 52–54, 88–91)* You tune a clarinet by pulling two or more joints apart slightly, or by using a different tuning barrel.

Tuning barrel See: *Barrel.*

Tuning ratios *(53)* The pitch differences between notes played with, or without the register key (E/B, F/C, and so on).

Tuning rings *(90)* Thin rings designed to fill up the groove that is formed inside the tube when tuning a clarinet.

Undercut toneholes See: *Toneholes.*

Upper register See: *Register, register key.*

Venting *(54)* Exactly how far the closed keys open when you press them affects the sound of your clarinet, but also its intonation. Also called *key opening.*

Window *(61, 62)* The opening of the mouthpiece.

TIPCODE LIST

The Tipcodes in this book offer easy access to short movies, photo series, soundtracks, and other additional information at www.tipbook.com. For your convenience, the Tipcodes in this Tipbook have been listed below.

Tipcode	Topic	Chapter	Pages
CLR-001	Fingers on the keys	2	5
CLR-002	The register key	2	7
CLR-003	Three registers	2	9
CLR-004	Ranges of four clarinets	2	13
CLR-005	A-concert pitch (440Hz)	5, 8	37, 88
CLR-006	Difference between 440 and 442Hz	5	37
CLR-007	'Problem notes'	5	57
CLR-008	Play on keys	5	59
CLR-009	German mouthpiece with cord	6	70
CLR-010	Adjusting underside reed	7	80
CLR-011	Cutting a reed	7	81
CLR-012	Using Dutch rush	7	81
CLR-013	Assembling a clarinet	8	85
CLR-014	Opening the bridge	8	86
CLR-015	Reed on mouthpiece	8	87
CLR-016	Tuning fork	8	88
CLR-017	Swab	8	92
CLR-018	Cleaning a pad	8	95
CLR-019	Sax, flute, oboe, and bassoon	11	110, 111
CLR-020	Making a clarinet	12	114
CLR-021	Manufacturing reeds	12	115

WANT TO KNOW MORE?

Tipbooks supply you with basic information on the instrument of your choice, and everything that has to do with it. Of course, there's a lot more to find on all subjects you come across on the previous pages. A selection of magazines, books and websites, as well as some background on the makers of the Tipbook series.

MAGAZINES

Some examples of magazines that offer plenty of information on clarinets and clarinet playing are:

- *The Clarinet* (US): International Clarinet Association, phone (630) 665-3602, membership@clarinet.org, www.clarinet.org.
- *Windplayer* (US), phone (310) 456-5813, info@windplayer.com, www.windplayer.com.
- *Australian Clarinet & Saxophone*, Queensland Clarinet & Saxophone Society, phone +61 (0)7 3341 8086, enquiries@clarinet-saxophone.asn.au, www.clarinet-saxophone.asn.au.
- *Clarinet & Saxophone* (UK): Clarinet and Saxophone Society of Great Britain, phone +44 (0)20 8979 6064, membership@cassgb.co.uk, www.cassgb.co.uk.

Activities

The International Clarinet Association, the European Clarinet and Saxophone Society (www.eurocass.org), and related organizations, which can be found in various countries, also organize meetings, seminars, workshops, and other activities for clarinetists.

BOOKS

Countless books have been written about clarinets and clarinetists. Those listed below cover the instrument itself and discuss other subjects, such as technique, history, and repertoire, at greater length.

- *Clarinet*, Jack Brymer (Yehudi Menuhin Music Guides, Kahn & Averill, UK, 1976; 259 pages; ISBN 1 871 08212 9).
- *Cambridge Companion to the Clarinet*, Colin Lawson (Cambridge University Press, 1995; 240 pages; ISBN 0 521 47066 8 [hardcover], 0 521 47668 2 [paperback]).
- *The Clarinet and Clarinet Playing*, David Pino (Dover Publication, New York, 1980; 306 pages; ISBN 0 486 40270 3).
- *Clarinet Acoustics*, O. Lee Gibson (Indiana University Press, 1994/1998; 84 pages; ISBN 0 253 21172 7).
- *The Complete Clarinet Player*, Paul Harvey (Music Sales Corporation, 1986; 192 pages; ISBN 0 711 91048 0).
- No longer in print, but still to be found in libraries is *The Clarinet; Some Notes on Its History & Construction*, F. Geoffrey Rendall; edition revised by Philip Bate (Ernest Benn Ltd., London, 1971; 206 pages; ISBN 0510-36701-1).

Reeds

Separate books have also been written about making and adjusting reeds. One is *Making Clarinet Reeds by Hand*, which can only be ordered from www.clarinetXpress.com.

INTERNET

On the Internet, you'll find countless sites for clarinetists, often with all kinds of links, articles, discussion groups, and FAQs (Frequently Asked Questions – and their answers). Two good sites with a lot of information and numerous links are The Online Clarinet Resource (www.ocr.sneezy.org) and The Clarinet Pages (www.sneezy.org/clarinet/index. html). Also check the websites mentioned above.

ABOUT THE MAKERS

Journalist, writer and musician Hugo Pinksterboer, (co)author of the Tipbook Series, has published hundreds of interviews, articles, and instrument, video, CD, and book reviews for national and international music magazines.

He wrote the reference work for cymbals (*The Cymbal Book*) and has written and developed a wide variety of manuals and courses, both for musicians and non-musicians.

Illustrator, designer, and musician Gijs Bierenbroodspot was the director for a wide variety of magazines, and developed numerous ad campaigns. While searching for information about saxophone mouthpieces, he got the idea for this series of books. He is responsible for the layout and the illustrations for all of the Tipbooks. He has also found a good mouthpiece, in the meantime.

ESSENTIAL DATA

In the event that your instrument is stolen or lost, or if you decide to sell it, it's always useful to have all the relevant data close at hand. Jot down those details on the following pages. Whether for the insurance company, for the police, for the person who buys it or just for yourself.

INSURANCE

Company:

Phone: Fax:

E-mail:

Agent:

Phone: Fax:

E-mail:

Policy number: Premium:

INSTRUMENTS AND ACCESSORIES

Brand and type:

Serial number: Price:

Date of purchase:

Purchased from:

Phone: Fax:

E-mail:

Brand and type:

Serial number: Price:

Date of purchase:

Purchased from:

Phone: Fax:

E-mail:

MOUTHPIECES

Brand and type:

Date of purchase: Price:

Purchased from:

Phone: Fax:

E-mail: